A GUIDE TO
SCOTCH
WHISKY

A GUIDE TO
SCOTCH WHISKY

MICHAEL BRANDER

Johnston & Bacon Publishers
Edinburgh & London

JB

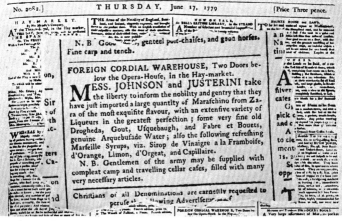

An extract from the *Morning Post*, June 17th, 1779 advertising
'usquebaugh'

Johnston & Bacon Publishers
35 Red Lion Square, London WC1R 4SG &
Tanfield House, Tanfield Lane, Edinburgh EH3 5LL

An imprint of
Cassell and Collier Macmillan Publishers Ltd.,
35 Red Lion Square, London WC1R 4SG
and at Sydney, Auckland, Toronto, Johannesburg
an affiliate of
Macmillan Inc., New York

First published 1975

ISBN 0 7179 4561 8 (paperback)

Printed in Great Britain by
The Camelot Press Ltd, Southampton

Contents

Acknowledgements

I would like to start by acknowledging my considerable debt of gratitude to the many people concerned in the Scotch Whisky industry who readily assisted me by providing information for this book. Without exception I found everyone I approached enormously willing to help. Since often several members of a group within the industry were helpful it would be invidious to select individuals by name. Furthermore, I must state that in no case are the firms or Associations within the industry to be held responsible for any views or comments I have put forward. I would like, however, to acknowledge particularly my indebtedness to the following: Messrs. Barton Distilling (Scotland) Limited; Arthur Bell and Sons Limited; The Distillers Company Limited; J. & G. Grant; Glenfarclas Distillery Limited; William Grant and Sons Limited; The Highland Distilleries Company Limited; The International Distillers and Vintners Limited; Invergordon Distillers Limited; Long John International Limited; North British Distillery Company; MacNab Distilleries Limited; Stanley P. Morrison and Company; The Pot-Still Malt Distillers Association; The Glenlivet Distillers Limited; Seagram Distillers Limited; Scottish and Newcastle Breweries Limited; The Scotch Whisky Association; Hiram Walker and Sons (Scotland) Limited; and finally to Mr. George Robertson of '37 Bar', Rose Street, Edinburgh, for letting us use his bar for the cover photograph; also to A. L. Hunter for taking the photograph.

In such a constantly developing industry it must be accepted that already quite a number of the facts stated may be out of date. I have, however, done my best to achieve accuracy and will be pleased to receive any corrections, additions, or suggestions for further editions; while making my apologies in advance for any errors which may have crept into the text, for which, as well as any omissions, I am entirely responsible.

◀ 'Slainte Mhath!' Good health! After piping in the haggis at a Burns supper, the pipe-major drinks to the health of the assembled company

Introduction

A visitor to Scotland may know little else about the country, but he, or she, whether rabid teetotaller, or fervent imbiber of alcohol, generally knows that it is the home of Scotch whisky. It is, perhaps, also not unusual if his, or her, knowledge begins and ends precisely there, for even the Scots themselves are often regrettably ignorant about their national drink.

Yet Scotch whisky is as much a part of the history of Scotland as Bannockburn or Flodden. It is as much a symbol of Scotland as the thistle or the kilt. Renowned in poetry and song, it is famed the world over as uniquely a product of Scotland. In fact, by law, Scotch whisky can only be made in Scotland. It is also the pure air and water, the peat and the soil of Scotland which contribute magically to the making of Scotch whisky.

When touring the Lowlands or the Highlands, the visitor cannot fail to see a number of distilleries. The characteristic pagoda type roof vents, the long low buildings beside a burn or river are often to be seen nestling inconspicuously in some out of the way spot, or close to a town.

Whether he will ever visit a distillery is another matter. Few people do, yet whisky distilleries have a lot to offer. They are generally in pleasant surroundings and close to beautiful countryside and each worker in a distillery takes a pride in his work, not least in the end product. They are as individual as the whiskies they produce, each of which differs from its neighbour.

Few distilleries are actively geared to tourism and only a minority are ready to open their doors to every tourist who wishes to visit them. Yet almost every distillery will be prepared to accept visitors with due warning and a suitable approach by letter, or telephone. It must be remembered, however, if you do visit a distillery whisky distilling has to come first. In such a competitive industry it could scarcely be otherwise.

This book is merely intended as a guide to indicate the origins and background of the Scotch whisky industry, so that the reader may enjoy his Scotch with the full knowledge of what he is drinking, where it comes from and who produced it. No attempt has been made to guide the reader's taste since taste is an essentially personal matter and what one man may like another may detest. In the end the reader will discover for himself that Scotch whisky distilling is not just another industry, that Scotch whisky is not just another drink, but that both are part of the national heritage, an integral part of Scotland itself.

Inspiring bold John Barleycorn!
What dangers thou canst make us scorn!
Wi' tipenny, we fear nae evil!
Wi' usquebae, we'll face the devil! *Robert Burns*

Of the Art of Distillation.

A hot Still.

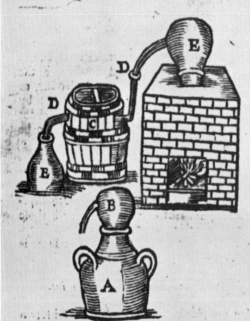

A, Sheweth the bottome which ought to be of Copper.

B, The Head.

C, The barrel filled with cold water to refrigerate and condensate the water and oyl that run through the pipe or worm that is put through it.

D, A pipe of brass or pewter, or rather a worm of Tin running through the barrel.

E, The Alembick set in the furnace with the fire under it.

How to make Aqua vitæ out of Beer.

Take of stale strong-beer, or rather, the grounds thereof, put it into a copper Still with a worm, distil it gently (or otherwise it will make the head of the Still fly up) and there will come forth a weak Spirit, which is called, low Wine: of which, when thou hast a good quantity, thou maist distil it again of it self. and there will come forth a good *Aqua vitæ*.

From *The Art of Distillation* (1664) by John French

Chapter 1

The origins and background of Scotch Whisky

Scotch Whisky is famous throughout the world and one of its fascinations is that there is so much individuality between the various distilleries and their whiskies. Even two stills side by side may produce quite distinctive whiskies. No one can really say why this is so and anyone who could provide the answer would undoubtedly be able to make his fortune! Yet, although many have tried, no one has ever succeeded. Whether it is in the water, or in the distilling process, or in the stills themselves that the difference lies, it is impossible to say.

The Scots have known the art of distilling a form of whisky from barley for well over a thousand years. The fact that alcohol has a lower boiling point than water forms the basis for all methods of distillation. Much preparation and skill is needed to produce the desired quality of spirit, but basically distillation starts when the fermented liquor is heated. The steam or vapour which rises from it contains alcohol and when taken off through a spout or pipe into the simplest form of a still these vapours condense as they cool into a liquid containing not only a high proportion of alcohol but also, at this stage, poisonous impurities.

Although the art of distillation has been known for so long in Scotland there was no written record of distilling processes until 1494. In the Exchequer records for that year there is a historic entry: 'Eight bolls of malt to Friar John Cor, wherewith to make aqua vitae.' Although Friar John Cor was using barley to make a form of whisky the term *aqua vitae*, or water of life, used loosely, could also mean spirit distilled from wine, or brandy. It was not until 1618, that there is the first mention of *Uisge beatha*, Gaelic for Water of Life, as being drunk at a chieftains's funeral in the Highlands. Thereafter it is clear whenever Uisge beatha is mentioned that it is spirit made from malted barley, or whisky, which is intended rather than brandy. From *Uisge* it was a simple transition to whisky.

A 17th-century still

Throughout the 17th century the distilling of whisky was steadily increasing throughout Scotland, most notably in the Highlands. So also was the skill and experience of the individual distillers. Without accurate instruments to measure quality and strength, great skill was needed to draw off the pure *middle cut* of spirit, avoiding the *foreshots*, or oily, poisonous higher alcohols at the start, and the later *feints*, or *aftershots*, containing lower alcohols at the end.

The measurement of the quality and strength of the spirit distilled, or what was eventually to be termed *proof*, was a very rough and ready business at this time. One of the commoner methods was to light a set amount and measure the liquid left behind. Another method was to add the spirit to gunpowder. If, when lit, the mixture exploded it was considered strong, or *over proof*, but if it was difficult to ignite it was considered weak, or *under proof*. If it burned steadily it was thought to be of the right strength and quality, or proof. A further method of estimating the strength and quality of the spirit was to shake it in a *proof phial*, or glass beaker, and then count the number of bubbles, or *beads*, formed, as these beads tend to form readily in strong grain spirit.

It was not until 1675 that Robert Boyle re-discovered Archimedes' invention of the hydrometer, which he termed

Transporting whisky 1890

'The New Essay Instrument'. It was described as 'a bubble furnished with a long and slender stem, which was to be put into several liquors to compare and estimate their specific gravities'. For this purpose 'Boyle's Bubble', as it was nicknamed, was quickly pressed into service by the Excise Officers. Although it was an improvement on the old methods it was not accurate to any fine degree. 'Boyle's Bubble' was soon being used, however, to decide whether a spirit was below or above proof and by 1688 the first Act had been introduced in England charging revenue duty on 'every gallon of brandy spirits, or aqua vitae, above proof . . . .' From this time on the duty in England was charged on strength rather than volume as had previously been the case. Scotland was not affected by this Act until the Union of the Parliaments in 1707 and the gradual introduction of English forms of taxation.

One of the taxes which caused considerable rioting on its introduction in Scotland in 1725 was the Malt Tax. Among its long-term results was a gradual change in the popular drinking tastes of the people of Scotland from ale to whisky, because the brewers were forced either to raise their prices to cover the extra tax, or else lower their quality. It also resulted in better whisky being produced illicitly in the Highlands

13

than was produced legally under licence in the Lowlands. In order to absorb the tax on malted barley the Lowland distillers were forced to use a mixture of unmalted grain and malted barley and produced a whisky of inferior quality. The Highlands, where unlicensed distillers predominated, produced a better whisky, even if entirely illicit, without payment of any tax.

By the last quarter of the 18th century the average whisky-still in Scotland had a seventy to eighty gallon capacity, but there were some large Lowland distillers with stills of over a thousand gallons. Particularly notable amongst these were Robert and John Haig at Leith, and the Stein brothers, James and John, at Clackmannan further up the Forth. In order to avoid the tax on malt, these distillers used oats, wheat, potatoes, turnips and other roots as far as possible as basic materials for distillation along with small quantities of malted barley to assist with fermentation. The resulting spirit was, of course, inferior to the product of pure malted barley. With a far larger demand in the more densely populated Lowland belt and with growing export sales to England, however, these Lowland distillers could afford to forgo quality in return for quantity.

The spirit exported to England was refined and redistilled in the form of gin and it was this competition from Scotland which roused the powerful gin distillers' lobby in England into action. In the 1780s as a result of their pressure, the English government started on a course of punitive tax legislation which was to result in a sharp division between Highland and Lowland distillers and eventually between the whiskies produced in each area. In order to simplify taxation, the idea was conceived of drawing an arbitrary line across Scotland, running roughly from Glasgow to Dundee, known as the *Highland Line*. North of this line distilleries were assessed at a lower level than to the south.

A tax was introduced in 1786 which was intended to equalise taxation between England and Scotland, thus checking exports of spirits to England. Unexpectedly, the Scots succeeded in absorbing the tax and still continued to export, whereupon the tax was increased yet again. The effect was immediate in the Lowlands, where the Haig brothers managed to survive, but the Stein brothers, who had been

A *The Still*	L *A Pewter Crane*
B *The Worm tub*	M *A Pewter Valencia*
C *The Pump*	N *Hippocrates bag or Flannel*
D *Water tub*	*Sleeve*
E *A Press*	O *Poker Fire-shovel Cole rake*
FFF *Tubs to hold the goods*	P *A Box of Bungs*
GGGG *Canns of different size*	Q *The Worm within the Worm tub*
H *A Wood Funnel with a iron nosel*	*mark'd with prick'd lines*
I *A large Vessel to put the Fains*	R *A Piece of Wood to keep down*
or after runnings	*the Head of the Still to*
K *Tin pump*	*prevent flying of*

Ph Fourdrinier Delin et Sculp

engaged in a price war with the English distillers, promptly went bankrupt. The English distillers heaved a sigh of relief and raised their prices again.

In 1781 an improvement on Boyle's hydrometer was introduced by Clarke and this was supposed to show by means of balls whether spirit was $\frac{1}{10}$th above proof, or $\frac{1}{10}$th below. In practice it proved highly erratic. Nor, of course, did this device affect the numerous and growing numbers of illicit distillers, especially in the Highlands. Despite further and frequent increases in taxation the principal result was merely fresh recruits to the ranks of the illicit distillers. The Excise Officers in general were either powerless or ineffectual and easily bribed.

In 1798 John Stein, one of the brothers who had been driven into bankruptcy in 1786, stated categorically at an enquiry into distilling in Scotland:

'It is not confined to great towns, or regular manufacturers, but spreads itself over the whole face of the country, and in every island from Orkneys to Jura. There are many who practise this art who are ignorant of every other, and there are distillers who boast that they make the best possible Whiskey [the spelling then common], who cannot read or write, and who carry on this manufacture in parts of the country where the use of the plough is unknown and where the face of the Exciseman is never seen. Under such circumstances, it is impossible to take into account its operations, it is literally to search for revenue in the woods or the mountains.'

The only answer the government could provide was to go on raising the taxes, doubling and redoubling them until from an annual licence of £1. 10s. per gallon of still-capacity in 1786 the tax had finally reached £162 in 1803. The ingenuity of the Scots distillers still managed to overcome these penal fiscal duties. Since it was a tax based on the capacity of the still the tax was spread more evenly the faster he could operate it. It was not unusual for stills of eighty gallons capacity to be worked off in three and a half minutes. In such circumstances the stills were soon worn out and many new still shapes were invented and tried out during this period. Indeed it was then that the modern shape of pot-still developed.

An illicit still in the Highlands in the 19th century

These enormous increases in taxation inevitably defeated their own ends and brought the law into disrepute since, with very few exceptions, everyone winked at illicit distilling. Those unable to afford the cost of frequent replacements for their stills were unable to continue distilling legally. This was a period when illicit distilling, or smuggling as it was termed, was widely accepted at all levels and it was often the case that it produced better whisky than was produced in many of the licensed stills.

The illicit distillers' methods were very simple. A sack of barley would be soaked in a bog, or burn, for two days before being spread out in a cave conveniently hidden in a mountainside. There, the barley would be allowed to germinate for about ten days. When it had reached a suitable stage, further growth would be checked by drying it over a peat fire. This produced the malted barley which was then put in a barrel or *mash-tun* and boiling water added. The resulting liquid was known as *wort* and when yeast had been added would be allowed to ferment. At this stage, the liquid now called *wash* would be ready for the pot-still. After being put through the still the mixture, then termed *low wines*, was still undrinkable until put through the still a second time when it finally emerged as raw malt whisky. If only one still was used it had to be thoroughly cleaned between the two operations or the spirit would taste very smoky. This process, carried out by these illicit distillers, had remained unaltered for centuries.

So widespread was illicit distilling that in the isolated area around Glenlivet it was said there were over 200 illicit stills operating. Indeed so common was distilling here and so good the product, that excellent whisky was often referred to as 'The Real Glenlivet' as the height of praise. George IV and Members of Parliament insisted on drinking Glenlivet whisky knowing full well that it was illicitly distilled!

Despite the fact that they were largely ineffectual against this universal illicit distilling, in one respect the Excise had vastly advanced. By 1818 they were using a new hydrometer invented by Bartholomew Sikes. This, at last, was an accurate instrument. By means of this they finally attained an accurate definition of proof as that 'which at a temperature of 51 degrees Fahrenheit weighs exactly $\frac{12}{13}$ths of an equal measure of distilled water'. By using a set of tables the operator could calculate an exact percentage of proof spirit from a sample

An officer of H.M. Customs and a distillery worker measure the strength of a sample of spirit with a Sikes hydrometer at Teananich Distillery, Alness, Highland Region

with the Sikes hydrometer. An instrument known as a saccharometer had also been developed which accurately measured the specific gravity of the wash, the fermented liquor prepared for the still. Despite these technical advances, the Excise Officers were still quite unable to overcome the problem of illicit distilling and, in 1823, Parliament finally introduced some much needed reforms.

They scrapped all the old legislation and high rates of duty, imposing a flat licence fee of £10 for all stills over forty gallons capacity and a duty of 2s. 3d. a gallon on whisky distilled. The idea was to encourage the honest distiller and provide him with an incentive to take out a licence. The immediate result was that the total consumption of tax-paid whisky which had dropped as low as two million gallons annually by 1825, had risen to 6 million gallons within two years. It is from this date that modern whisky distilling in Scotland may be said to have started.

In 1828 Robert Stein, a member of the Stein distilling family, now intermarried with the Haigs, introduced a new type of continuous operating still. It was so named because unlike the pot-still it did not require two operations to produce the raw spirit. It was a complicated process, but a Stein still was built at the Haig distillery at Cameron Bridge in 1830. In 1831, however, Aeneas Coffey, the ex-Inspector General for Ireland, invented a much simpler form of continuous still for which he was granted a patent in 1832. Whisky distilled by this process became known as patent-still whisky, or grain whisky, as opposed to malt whisky distilled through two pot stills in the time-honoured way.

The patent-still immediately introduced a new element into whisky distilling. Whereas there had been an increasing tendency for the Lowland whisky distiller to use little malted barley, with the patent-still he now required even less. He used rye, oats, or maize when available and only a small quantity of malted barley. The difference between the Highland whisky which was mainly malt and the Lowland whisky which was mostly grain whisky was even more sharply accentuated by this new invention than it had been before. The patent-still ushered in a new era in the making of whisky and both grain and malt whisky have their own place in producing the world famous Scotch Whisky.

Cutting peat

A sample of barley after it has been steeped, germinated and kiln-dried

Chapter 2

The mechanics of Scotch Whisky

With the development of the Coffey Patent-still and the introduction of the 1823 Act, whisky distilling in Scotland passed quickly from an almost wholly domestic craft into a steadily growing industry. Whereas previously, quite often, the entire process from making the malt to the final distilling was in the hands of one individual, now specialists began to take charge of each phase of the larger scale industrial operation. The process, however, was a gradual one and it was not really until the latter part of the 19th century that the industry had reached this stage of growth.

In some modern distillery complexes, a patent-still and pot-stills may be found working in virtually one unit. The two stills and processes are very different, however, and the next few pages trace the pot-still and patent-still methods of making whisky.

Pot-Stills

The secret of making malt whisky in pot-stills in the Highlands has always depended not only on the people concerned and their unrivalled inherited knowledge, but also on the very countryside itself. The real secret lies in the supreme softness and purity of the Highland water and the subtle aroma imparted by the Highland peat used in the distilling process. The peat is composed largely of heather and mosses compressed over the centuries into a fibrous mass, and it burns with a sweet smelling turfy reek. It is cut from the peat beds into blocks the size of a large brick and the peat stacks, drying in the summer winds, are a feature of the Highland scenery.

At one time, malt whisky in the Highlands was only made from the finest Highland barley, such as was produced in the Laigh of Moray. Today, however, there is not enough barley produced in the Highlands to keep pace with the amount of whisky distilled. Much of the barley now used comes from England, Europe and even Australia.

At the Imperial Distillery, Carron, Grampian Region, skilled raking (foreground) and turning (background) of the grain ensures uniform germination

It is common modern practice for barley to arrive at a distillery already malted, but where this is not the case, when the barley arrives it is put through a dressing machine to remove any impurities prior to being stored ready for use. When required it is then placed in large, low tanks, known as *steeps*, which generally hold over half a ton each. The grain is soaked in water in these for about 57 hours. Traditionally it is then spread evenly but thickly on the floor of the malt barn, a long low-roofed building, where it is turned daily with broad wooden shovels known as *shiels* and left to germinate. This allows the sugar from the starch in the barley to be released. The modern method of doing this is to put the barley into mechanical drums known as Saladin boxes or into concrete or metal containers where it is turned by mechanical forks.

When the desired stage has been reached, germination is then checked by drying the malt in a kiln over peat fires. The kilns, with their pagoda-style heads, are perhaps the commonest feature associated with the average pot-still distillery. Beneath them the malted barley is dried on perforated sheets of iron over a peat fire. This gives malt

The distinctive pagoda-shaped chimneys of a
malt whisky distillery

whisky the distinctive flavour of the peat smoke, which can
still be tasted in the end product.

The malted barley is then usually left for a period of about
six weeks before being put through the mill and bruised to
release the starch. It is then put in the mash tun, which is a
large circular container. Mash tuns may vary in size from
about 1,000 gallons capacity to around 5,000 or more. Here, the
malted barley is mixed with hot water and stirred to dissolve
the sugar in the mash. The liquid obtained is a sweet-tasting
non-alcoholic mixture, known as wort. This is strained off
and hot water is again poured into the mash tun, and the
process repeated. The mashing process may take as much as
ten hours or more. The grains left behind are turned into a
form of cattle feed known as *draff*.

The wort is then passed through a cooling process and into
the fermentation vats, known as *washbacks*. In these large vats,
varying in size from around 2,000 gallons to well over 10,000,
the wort has yeast added to it and the fermentation process
begins. After a few days, the resulting wash has become the
first weak stage of alcoholic liquor, which in the end will

The mash tun at the Talisker Distillery, Isle of Skye

As the yeast attacks the sugar in the malt extract at the Aberfeldy Distillery, Tayside Region, the whole body of the 'wash' bubbles and boils. Fermentation takes from 36 to 44 hours.

An apprentice at the Waverley Vintners Cooperage in Leith undergoes the 500 year old traditional initiation ceremony for fully-fledged coopers

become whisky. This liquor is now ready to enter the final stage, the stills themselves.

The first of the two stills into which the wash is fed is known as the *wash-still*. In this vast copper container it is brought to the boil and the vapours are conducted through a long spout to the *worm*, or copper coil, immersed in cold water. The ensuing liquor is known as low wines and is now ready for distillation in the second still, the *spirit-still*. The liquor, at this stage, however, is quite undrinkable.

In the spirit-still the same process takes place with the vapour led through the coil, but thereafter the liquor distilled is run through a glass fronted container, known as the *Distiller's Safe*. This has hydrometers behind glass, and the *Stillman* in charge of the distilling process at this stage can check the strength of the spirits as they come from the coil. It is necessary to separate the foreshots, or undesirable raw spirits in the first run of spirit, from the main run. It is also necessary to cut out the poisonous after shots from the main run and it is in this last operation that much of the skill of making good malt whisky lies.

From the still, the raw whisky is run into large containers known as *vats*, where it is temporarily stored before being drawn off into casks. Coopers are in charge of the casks, though most of their work today is concerned with checking and repairing where required, rather than making casks. Indeed the best casks for storing whisky are considered to be old sherry butts and it is from these in many cases that the whisky gains both colour and flavour. Many distilleries, however, re-use the staves of casks from the U.S.A. which have been used for storing whisky there and by U.S. law may not be used a second time. It is in these oak casks that the whisky will then mature for a given number of years. By law, it has to mature at least three years, but generally nearer eight or ten depending on the requirements of the distillery. Some whiskies are known to be quick maturing and others late, and much depends on the locality, the water and the distilling methods. Each malt whisky differs from the next, even those from neighbouring stills; therein lies its charm and attraction.

Over all the latter part of the distilling process, from the wash to the raw spirit and onwards, the Excise Officer is always in the background. There are only some 800 Excise officers in the northern area bounded by a line running roughly across through Aberdeen, nor are the distilleries their

Whisky maturing at the Imperial Distillery, Carron, Grampian Region

only task. They have the usual Customs and Excise work in addition, they investigate wrecks and coastlines, as well as looking for illicit distilling. However, today, they would be more likely to find illicit stills in Birmingham or Manchester than north of the Highland Line.

Patent-Stills

The patent-still grain distillery is very different from the pot-still malt distillery. Almost all the patent-still distilleries are to be found in the Lowlands. Since they are not tied to any particular source of water they are not found in out of the way Highland glens. They do not have the distinctive roofs of the pot-still malt distillery and look more like any other industrial factory.

Since the patent-still can operate continuously, the mash tuns and the fermentations vats are on a much larger scale than those needed for the pot-still malt distillery. The space required for storage of maize, rye or other grain used in the process is also correspondingly much greater. On the other hand, because the need for malted barley is much less in patent-stills it is generally obtained from outside. Therefore,

At Glen Elgin Distillery, Elgin, Grampian Region, the resident Excise Officer watches the filling of new whisky into casks for maturing

neither malting barns nor malt kilns are really required, or only on a very small scale.

Inside the distillery the patent-still consists of two large cylindrical copper columns about forty feet high, joined together at the top by a junction pipe. One of these columns is known as the *analyser* and the other as the *rectifier*. They are each sub-divided by perforated copper plates into a number of horizontal compartments.

The distilling process is started by pressure-boiling the grain in vast containers to produce a breakdown of the starch. A small amount of malted barley is added during the mashing process to increase the sugar content. Then comes the large-scale fermentation before pumping the liquid into the still.

A jet of steam passes through the columns and when the wash enters the still it is first pumped through a coiled pipe running down the entire rectifier column. This effectively cools the column while heating the wash before it is directed into the top of the analyser column. At this stage it meets the upward jet of steam rising through the perforated plates. Since alcohol boils and evaporates at a lower temperature than water, as the wash slowly drips downwards through each succeeding compartment the alcohol rises with the steam. The steam is diverted into the base of the rectifier column and continues to rise, steadily condensing on the cooling plates of each compartment and cooled by the fresh wash being pumped downwards. By this method the purest alcohol rises to the top while the heavier impure higher and lower alcohols condense lower down, having a lower boiling point. They are then drawn off for re-distillation and the end-product is nearly pure alcohol. Patent-still grain whisky is less subject to variation than the pot-still malt whisky and it also matures much faster.

It has, however, by law, to mature for three years although it is not usually matured in casks for much longer than this. Most of the patent-still whisky is used for blending with malt whiskies to produce the world famous Scotch Whiskies. A great deal of skill and care is needed to produce these fine blends and some are matured again in casks before being bottled. It is essential that the correct amount of time is given for maturing because when a whisky has been bottled it does not change greatly.

Chapter 3

The blending of Scotch Whisky

Not surprisingly there was considerable opposition to the patent-still from the pot-still malt whisky distillers. Despite this, however, the production of the patent-still grain whisky increased. From 1830 to 1850 the production of malt whisky continued to be greater than that of grain whisky, but during this time the annual amount of grain whisky increased and, by 1860 it was around 17% greater than malt whisky production.

The reason for this was not the greater popularity of grain whisky as opposed to malt. It was entirely due to the custom, of mixing grain and malt whiskies in a process which became known as blending. This began during the 1850's and was possibly copied from the habit of the brandy manufacturers of mixing brandies. It was reputedly Andrew Usher & Company, the agents for the sale of 'The Glenlivet', who introduced the first blend in 1853. Initially the mixture of various malts was known as a *blend*, whereas a mixture of malt and grain whisky was simply termed a *mixture*. Gradually as other merchants and wholesalers began selling various mixtures and blends the term, blend, came to cover both malt mixed with grain as well as the combinations of malt whiskies. Since it increased demand for both grain and malt whiskies the distillers raised no objection.

The process was gradual. Between 1855 and 1870 the blends became a generally accepted feature and the art of blending grew rapidly more important as the benefits of having a reliable and consistently even flavour sold under a brand name became apparent. Merchants and wholesalers now began to gain control of the industry, forcing the malt distillers to hold stocks of whisky in bond at their convenience. The grain distillers were less affected since they were able to produce considerable quantities more or less at will, whereas the pot-still malt distillers were forced to follow the slow routine of distilling in two pot-stills.

One result of the devastation of the wine crops and vineyards in Europe by the insect, *Phylloxera Vastatrix* towards the end of the 19th century was that brandy was no longer available. The English turned to Scotch whisky instead. Scotch whisky, blended from malt and grain whiskies, became the most popular drink not only in Britain, but also increasingly throughout the world wherever the Scots or English might be found. Certain outstanding names and blends such as *Buchanan's, Dewars, Johnnie Walker, Queen Anne* or *Vat 69* became almost synonymous with Scotch whisky.

There can be no doubt, however, that a great deal of deception was practised during this period. The advantage of being able to utilise the cheaper grain whisky in conjunction with the more expensive malt whisky was not overlooked. A great many cheap blends were sold to ignorant customers in the south as pure malt whisky, or as fine blended Glenlivet, or under similar names.

An industry cannot avoid being affected by such malpractices and, inevitably, great harm was done when an apparently respectable firm of blenders and wholesalers was found to be guilty of such conduct. The firm of Pattisons Limited went bankrupt in 1891 and the two owners, Walter and Robert Pattison, were imprisoned after it was found they had been mixing raw grain whisky at $11\frac{1}{2}d$. a gallon with a minimal quantity of malt whisky and selling it as 'Fine Glenlivet' at 8s. 6d. a gallon.

Today, the Scotch Whisky Association acts as the watchdog of the industry and aims to prevent malpractices which can harm the industry. However, there are a few distillers or wholesalers, possibly controlled by interests outside the whisky industry, who occasionally sell *young blends* abroad as 'Fine blended Scotch Whisky'. It is difficult to check, since the blends used are above the legal maturing limit of three years, but are still very immature and do not merit the title of 'fine'. To avoid this a customer should always buy a reputable blend rather than save a few pence by buying something cheaper.

The modern term for mixing single whiskies of the same kind, whether grain or malt, is *vatting*. Both the art of vatting and that of blending have now reached a very high degree of science and exactitude. Blending in particular is an essential, indeed vital, part of the industry. The blender may mix as

many as thirty or more different malts and grain whiskies to achieve his perfect blend. He does this by *nosing* or smelling, each in turn, never by tasting. The various constituents which have been matured in casks are then mixed in vats and finally may be stored in casks again to blend and to allow them further time to mature. The consistency of the quality of the major blends is a compliment to the powers of the blenders concerned.

Some of the best-known vatted malt whiskies are, *Findlaters Mar Lodge, Highland Fusilier, Glencoe, Glenleven, Hudson's Bay, Old Bannockburn* and *Pride of Strathspey*. Unlike the limited number of vatted malts there are well over 2,000 blends and the Appendix lists some of the more notable.

Chapter 4

Famous names in Scotch Whisky

The Scotch whisky industry has experienced many changes, problems and pressures from the whisky boom in the last quarter of the 19th century to the decline of the industry through the First World War, the Prohibition in the U.S.A., and the adverse effects of the Second World War. In the days of the boom a newly-built distillery could recoup its initial investment within a few years, but, with the crash of the Pattison brothers in 1898 and the outbreak of war in 1914, many distillers and firms were forced to close. It was these difficulties heightened by Prohibition that led to the growth of combines such as the 'Big Five' and the Distillers Company Limited. After the Second World War the industry began to recover and has continued to expand and develop.

Despite difficulties in the past, several names have remained supreme and synonymous with Scotch Whisky. In the following brief backgrounds to these companies, which were often guided by one person, the changing fortunes and trends in the industry itself are apparent.

The Glenlivet
The first distiller to take out a licence under the 1823 Act was George Smith of Upper Drumin in Glenlivet, the area most famed throughout Scotland for the quality of its illicitly distilled whisky. His example was quickly followed by others elsewhere, but two would-be distillers who took out licences in his area were soon cowed by threats to burn their distilleries about their ears and withdrew. Smith had also received such threats but refused to pay any attention to menaces of this kind from his neighbours and erstwhile friends, illicit distillers to a man. He armed himself with a pair of hair-trigger pistols and vowed to give as good as he got. He deserved to be successful and successful he was.

In 1860, in conjunction with his son John Gordon Smith, trading as G. & J. G. Smith, he scrapped his old distilleries and opened up a much larger one at Minmore in Glenlivet.

Already the fame of the Glenlivet whisky had spread far and wide and demand was such that numerous distilleries within a twenty mile radius claimed to distil 'Glenlivet' whisky. So many traded on the known excellence of the name that the Smiths prevailed on their landlord the Duke of Richmond and Gordon to write as follows:

'November 6 1865. The District of Glenlivet, a part of the Gordon property in Scotland belongs to me. My tenants George and John Gordon Smith, whose distillery of malt whisky is called "The Glenlivet Distillery" are the only distillers in the Glenlivet District—Richmond.'

Even this failed to prevent their name being used and, in 1880, after his father's death in 1871, John Gordon Smith decided to take the misuse of the name Glenlivet by other distillers to law. By a legal settlement other distilleries were allowed to hyphenate the name Glenlivet to their name by agreement with George & J. G. Smith and, in the end, as many as twenty-five applied to do so, though some were over twenty miles away.

The present chairman of the firm, since 1921, is Captain William Smith Grant who is a great grandson of the founder of 'The Glenlivet'. Until the late 1960's they were the only distillery in Glenlivet, but although there are others now, the use of the title, 'The Glenlivet' is still theirs alone by right.

Grant

Grant is a familiar name in distilling, especially in the district of Moray on Speyside, the home of the Grants. In 1840 the Glen Grant distillery was founded by the brothers John and James Grant, distillers of the famous Glen Grant malt whisky. The Glenfarclas-Glenlivet distillery founded in 1836 by Robert Hay but taken over in 1865 by John and George Grant, father and son, trading as J. & G. Grant, Limited. The firm still has a George Grant as Managing Director today.

Another notable example is that of the Glenfiddich distillery owned by William Grant. He built the distillery with his own hands in 1887 and since his death it has been owned and managed by his sons and grandsons. The noted Longmorn-Glenlivet distillery is another which owes its present distinction to Cyril and Len Grant. These are but a few of the numerous examples within the industry.

Old *Glen Grant* Label

There is a story about two rival distillery owners named Grant who encountered each other at a mutual Grant relation's funeral on a bitterly cold day. They were waiting for the funeral procession to arrive at the graveside when one offered the other his flask and remarked:

'Ye may as well have a dram, ye'll not often get the opportunity of anything as good.'

The other took a good swallow and returned the flask poker-faced with the reply:

'Man that's just what I required. I'd have brought my own flask, but I don't want it said I smelled of whisky at the funeral.'

Distillers Company Limited

This great industrial empire owed its being originally to a 'trade arrangement' entered into by six Lowland grain distillers in 1856 when it seemed as if competition could only bring them all to bankruptcy. Perhaps the most notable name in that combination was that of John Haig and Company.

After nine years this Trade Arrangement was re-formed with a slightly different membership. The advantages of centralisation of control and amalgamation of interests were so obvious that finally in 1877 the following grain distillers merged to form a single company: John Bald & Company, Carsebridge Distillery, Alloa; John Haig & Company, Cameron Bridge Distillery, Fife; M. Macfarlane & Company, Fort Dundas Distillery, Glasgow; MacNab Brothers & Company, Glenochil Distillery, Menstrie; Robert Mowbray, Cambus Distillery, Alloa; Stewart & Company, Kirkliston Distillery, Lothian. They formed the Distillers Company based in Edinburgh and are generally known as the D.C.L. It was significant that John Haig, wishing to preserve their identity, formed a new company in Fife.

The D.C.L. owed its phenomenal expansion and success mainly to one man, William Ross. He joined the firm in 1878 at the age of 16 as a junior clerk, and combined mathematical skill with vision and courage as well as an ability to deal with people. By 1900 he had become Managing Director, a post he was to occupy until 1931. The vast expansion of the D.C.L. from 1900 onwards was almost entirely due to him.

With the outbreak of the First World War in 1914 there was an increasingly uncertain economic climate for the entire whisky industry until well into the 1930s. Ross was sufficiently far-sighted to see that the only solution lay in amalgamation and mergers. He was determined to achieve mergers with the 'Big Five' as they were known, the firms of Buchanan, Dewar, Haig, Mackie and Walker. In 1919 the D.C.L. successfully achieved the first merger with the firm of Haig & Haig, continuing to run John Haig as a subsidiary until 1924 when it was also merged.

In 1915 Buchanan and Dewar had themselves merged to form a single firm, known as Buchanan-Dewar, with a view to withstanding the uncertainties created by the war. In 1925 Ross persuaded both Buchanan-Dewar and the firm of John Walker to join him at the conference table with a view to discussing a merger. The result was a triumph for Ross. The merger took place and he was unanimously appointed chairman of the board. Although Sir Peter Mackie, the highly individualistic chairman of Mackie's White Horse Distillers Limited, refused any approaches from the D.C.L. in his lifetime the firm was amalgamated shortly after his death in 1927. With control of around 40% of the industry Ross had achieved his ambition to make the D.C.L. the most powerful combine of its kind in Britain.

'Big Five'

Buchanan
The whisky industry has had its share of outstanding characters, not least among them the 'Big Five' themselves. Such men as James Buchanan, subsequently created Lord Woolavington, would have made their mark in any sphere. He went to London in 1879 as a whisky salesman for Charles Mackinlay, the blenders and merchants. Five years later in 1884 he started on his own with very little backing beyond his remarkable ability as a salesman and his acute business acumen. He was always faultlessly turned out in a frock coat and top hat and had immense charm and personality. Marketing a light blended whisky suitable for southern tastes, he named it *Buchanan's* and sold it in a bottle with a distinctive

Add a little smoothness to your day.

A recent advertisement for Dewar's *White Label* whisky

black and white label. Within a year of his arrival, all London, including the House of Commons, was drinking his *Black and White* whisky. He never looked back.

Inevitably such a figure created his own legend. In return for a large contribution to party funds, he was offered the title of Lord Woolavington by Lloyd George in 1920, and, not trusting the Liberal Leader, signed the cheque 'Woolavington'. He was a member of the Jockey Club and a keen sportsman. He bred and raced his own horses, and twice won the Derby, in 1920 and 1926. He lived on until 1935 when he died at the ripe old age of 86.

Dewar

John Dewar, set up as a whisky merchant in Perth in 1846, and was one of the first to sell whisky in bottles rather than in the cask. He died in 1880, leaving his eldest son, John Alexander, as manager of the business. He was joined by his younger brother Thomas Robert in 1884. Within a year, the irreverent, witty and utterly irrepressible young 'Tommy' Dewar had made his mark on London by playing the bagpipes at the Brewer's Show. The Committee tried to have him thrown out but he continued to play regardless and the publicity was tremendous. The orders soon followed.

The elder brother, John, was Lord Provost of Perth and M.P. before being made Lord Forteviot in 1916 as just reward for his public services. Thomas was always in the public eye and, though made Lord Dewar in 1919, was known far and wide familiarly as 'Tommy' Dewar. He was a member of the Jockey Club and a keen racehorse and greyhound owner and won the Waterloo Cup, the supreme prize in Coursing in 1915. He and his brother made a powerful team and they assisted in opening up the English market when the industry's survival depended on finding fresh markets. The two brothers both died in 1930.

Johnnie Walker

Another name familiar the world over is that of Johnnie Walker. The firm started in 1820 when the original John Walker opened a grocer's shop in Kilmarnock. The shop developed into a whisky merchant's business in the 1850s when his son Alexander joined him and by 1880 the firm was prospering to the extent that Alexander, by this time in sole control, decided to open a London office. He soon attracted attention by using his own specially built carriage and a superb matched pair of horses instead of travelling the normal businessman's way, by hansom cab. As with Buchanan and Dewar his showmanship brought in custom. By 1866 he was able to form a company with his sons George and John in the name of John Walker & Sons Limited.

It was a clever young newcomer to the firm, James Stevenson, later created Lord Stevenson, together with Alec Walker, a grandson of the original John, who promoted the now famous *Johnnie Walker* blend in the first decade of the 20th century. Unfortunately, Stevenson died quite young but Sir Alec Walker, as he became, lived on until the 1950s living up to the famous slogan of the firm 'Johnnie Walker . . . still going strong'.

Of the two, however, it was Stevenson who left his abiding mark on the Scotch whisky industry. During the 1914–18 War, and when Prohibition in the U.S.A. appeared likely, he persuaded Lloyd George to pass an act instituting a two years' minimum maturing period in bond. This was soon extended

Whisky advertising at the turn of the century. An early use of bus sides for advertisements. Note the bus at the bottom right and the one next to Eros in Piccadilly Circus

to three years and this Act still remains in force. It has done nothing but good for the industry, since the sale of immature spirits cannot help having an adverse effect.

Mackie

Yet another of the big names in the formative years of the whisky industry was that of Sir Peter Mackie, famous for promoting his 'White Horse' blend. He proudly proclaimed that his motto was 'Nothing is Impossible' and did his best to live up to it. Those who were not prepared to call him something a good deal stronger nicknamed him 'Restless Peter'. Nor did he restrict his energies to the whisky industry. He was a keen public speaker and opposed the Liberals on every platform. Independent, egotistical and forthright he resisted, as already mentioned, all the approaches made by the D.C.L. during his lifetime.

Haig

Perhaps the oldest name associated with whisky is, of course, that of Haig. This company dates back as far as the 17th century. The most famous member of the family was Field Marshal Lord Haig, both lauded and blamed for his part in the First World War. He was appointed a director of the Haig distillery at Cameron Bridge in 1894 and continued his family interest in distilling throughout his army career. In acknowledgement of this he was appointed a director of the D.C.L. in 1922 until his death in 1928.

To the public at large, however, the name Haig will always be associated with their advertising. Although their earlier advertisement 'D'ye ken John Haig' may now be forgotten, their modern version 'Don't be vague, ask for Haig', is still one of the most potent selling slogans in the industry. Even the most fervent teetotaller must have noticed this pithy phrase.

Chapter 5

Why Scotch is unique to Scotland

The climate, the purity of the water, the aroma of the peat and the intrinsic knowledge acquired over the centuries all combine to make Scotch whisky inimitable anywhere else in the world. Attempts have been made to copy all the factors involved and to make Scotch whisky elsewhere without success. Despite enormous expense and apparent duplication of all the necessary factors the result is never the same. A Scots distiller commented after sampling a Japanese whisky:

'If you drank it all day and all night you might end up by thinking it was like Scotch whisky . . . but by then you might be dead.'

As well as this, it is illegal to make *Scotch* whisky anywhere but in Scotland. Any attempt to sell spirit distilled in another country as Scotch may result in a court case and heavy damages. The Scotch Whisky Association, guardian of Scotch Whisky interests around the world, is ever alert to such transgressions of the law.

It started with a court case which caused an enormous furore in 1905. At that time, the rivalry between malt and grain whisky distillers was still bitter. The malt distillers with their more expensive and slower pot-still methods could not rival the output of the grain distillers with their patent-still methods. The malt distillers claimed that grain whisky was not truly Scotch whisky.

The issue was suddenly brought into the public eye when Islington Borough Council issued summonses against several publicans on the grounds that they had sold whisky 'not of the nature, substance and quality demanded by the purchaser'.

The magistrate before whom the case was held went into the evidence very thoroughly and the matter took three months to settle. He then gave judgement against the grain distillers, ruling that 'Whisky should consist of spirit distilled in a pot-still, derived from malted barley, mixed, or not, with unmalted barley and wheat, or either of them.'

An appeal was promptly lodged but the Clerkenwell Quarter Sessions, the only Court of Appeal with a bench of lay magistrates, was unable to reach agreement. The original verdict therefore remained unaltered, but obviously the position could not be allowed to remain there, with no clear definition of what did constitute whisky in law.

The malt distillers and the grain distillers began to seek a compromise since the fight was truly in the interests of neither. They appealed to the government and in 1908 a Royal Commission was formed and sat for seventeen months hearing many expert witnesses. Among them were those who proved that the patent-still method of making whisky produced similar residues to those of the pot-still, only less in quantity therefore purer. Others made the point that most blends were of 50% malt and 50% grain and that this produced a light blended whisky which was preferred in England to the heavier malts.

In 1909 the Commission declared: 'Our general conclusion . . . is that "whiskey" (the common spelling of the time) is a spirit obtained by distillation from a mash of cereal grains saccharified by the diastase of malt: that "Scotch whiskey" is whiskey, as above defined distilled in Scotland. . . . We have received no evidence to show that the form of the still has any necessary relationship to the wholesomeness of the spirit produced.'

It was a triumph for the grain distillers and the D.C.L. in particular since they had organised and marshalled the evidence on the issue. The Commission had defined Scotch whisky as being a whisky distilled in Scotland. This was vitally important for the entire industry. It eventually became incorporated in Statute Law (as late as 1952) and thus honoured by governments throughout the world. It therefore more or less assured the future of the entire industry.

At the time, this was not apparent to all concerned and the division between malt and grain distillers seemed as deep as ever. The importance of the Royal Commission's findings were only fully appreciated much later, during the early years of the American Prohibition introduced in 1920.

A German firm in Mainz shipped their own spirit to the U.S.A. labelled 'Black and White Horse Whisky'. The firm of James Logan Mackie, producers of the noted *White Horse* blend took them to court. They won their case and Scotch whisky had won an important international victory.

The formation of the Whisky Association which also included Irish Whiskey interests, in 1917 brought a measure of unity to the industry. Its formation was brought about by the pressures incurred in wartime conditions. Its successor, the Scotch Whisky Association, representing only Scotch whicky interests, was also formed during the wartime conditions of the Second World War.

Founded in 1942, the object of the Scotch Whisky Association is to protect and promote the interests of the Scotch whisky trade generally both at home and abroad.

GRAIN DISTILLERIES

Orkneys
Kirkwall
ISLANDS

Thurso

Wick

North Sea

Lewis

Ullapool

Invergordon

Elgin

Isle of Skye
Carbost

HIGHLAND

Inverness

GRAMPIAN

Loch Ness

Aberdeen

Atlantic Sea

Fort William   Ben Nevis

Lochside

TAYSIDE

Dundee

Oban

Perth

Cameronbridge

FIFE

STRATHCLYDE

CENTRAL

North of Scotland   Carsebridge

Isle of Jura

Dumbarton

Stirling

Cambus

Caledonian

Edinburgh

Isle of Islay

Port Dundas

North British   LOTHIAN

Glasgow

Berwick

Strathclyde   Moffat

Port Ellen

BORDERS

Kintyre   Campbeltown

Ayr

Girvan

DUMFRIES & GALLOWAY

Dumfries

Stranraer

Region	TAYSIDE
Town	● Thurso
Distillery	● Lochside

Chapter 6

The whereabouts of Grain Whisky

There are at present fourteen Scottish grain whisky distilleries in Scotland compared with around a hundred and seventeen malt whisky distilleries. The process of continuous distillation which is possible with the Coffey Patent-Still in a grain distillery as opposed to the double distillation required by the pot-still method of distillation for malt whisky, means that the output of these few grain whisky distilleries, is still easily in excess of the malt pot-still distilleries.

Almost all their output goes into the many blends of Scotch whisky available although there is one grain whisky available in bottle and that is *Choice Old Cameron Brig*, distilled at Cameronbridge in Fife. As at 1974 there were the following grain distilleries in Scotland listed by regions in alphabetical order. The name of the distillery is shown in bold type and the geographical location in brackets alongside for easy reference. The main Regions are also indicated.

Central Region

Cambus   (in Cambus, 2 miles west of Alloa)
Close to the upper reaches of the Firth of Forth, this distillery was established in a small way in 1806 by John Mowbray on the site of an old mill. The enterprise prospered and grew enormously, especially after the introduction of the patent-still in the 1830's. In 1877 Robert Mowbray of Cambus, known as the 'Subtle Mowbray', was one of the founder members of the D.C.L. The distillery is controlled today by the Scottish Grain Distillers Limited, a subsidiary of the D.C.L.

Carsebridge   (about half a mile north east of Alloa)
This distillery was built about 1800 as a malt pot-still distillery by John Bald. In 1845 it passed to his son John, by which time it had changed over to grain distilling, using the patent-still. By 1877 John Bald & Company of Carsebridge, were one of

the founder members of the D.C.L. It was possibly due to this move that the Managing Director at that time was called the 'Politic Bald'. The distillery is now controlled by the Scottish Grain Distillers Limited.

North of Scotland   (adjacent to Cambus)
The North of Scotland distillery was founded in 1958 by G. P. Christie. It is now controlled by the North of Scotland Distilling Company Limited, in which the Christie family remain the major share holders.

Fife

Cameronbridge (at Windygates, just north of Buckhaven)
This distillery was established in 1824 by John Haig. A Stein patent-still was introduced in 1828 and a Coffey Still in 1832. In 1877 John Haig & Company, Cameronbridge, were founder members of the D.C.L. The Company is now controlled by the Scottish Grain Distillers Limited and distils the only grain whisky available in bottle in Scotland, *Choice old Cameron Brig*.

Highland Region

Ben Nevis   (just north of Fort William)
This patent-still grain distillery beside Ben Nevis was added in 1878 to the malt distillery already in existence. It was established by P. McDonald, son of the famed 'Long John' McDonald. In due course the distillery complex had to be greatly extended due to the ever increasing demand for the blend, *Long John's Dew of Ben Nevis* and it is now controlled by the Ben Nevis Distillery (Fort William) Limited.

Invergordon   (halfway between Dingwall and Tain)
Invergordon was once famed as a naval base. It is now best known for its industrial development, of which Invergordon Distillery is no small part. One of the largest distilleries in Europe, it was built in the 1950's at a cost of over £2,000,000. It is the most northerly grain distillery in Britain and part of a considerable distilling complex controlled by Invergordon Distillers Limited.

Lothian Region

North British (Wheatfield Road, Edinburgh)
This distillery was established in 1885 when a number of leading blenders decided that it was in the best interests of the Scotch Whisky industry to ensure an alternative source of supply of grain whisky. This, in fact, was a grain distillery run by the industry for the industry, providing an independent source of grain whisky for blending. Shareholders were restricted to wholesale whisky merchants and shares could be pre-empted on retirement or death of a shareholder. It is significant that, although at one time there were a number of distilleries in Edinburgh, today only the North British and the Caledonian Distillery survive. Greatly modernised and expanded, the North British Distillery continues to flourish and is still controlled by the North British Distillery Company Limited.

Caledonian (near to Haymarket Station, Edinburgh)
This distillery was established in 1855 by Menzies & Company and was acquired by the D.C.L. in 1884. It was ideally situated for rail transport and also for the Forth & Clyde Canal before its closure. It became the centre of technological improvements and the second largest distillery in Britain. It is now controlled by the Scottish Grain Distillers Limited.

Strathclyde Region

Dumbarton (Dumbarton)
The Dumbarton distillery stands fourteen stories high and close to the Dumbarton Rock, itself a landmark on the Clyde.

Visitors are welcome at the distillery which is owned by Hiram Walker and Sons (Scotland) Limited. This Canadian firm built the distillery in 1937 on the site of McMillan's Shipyard and it has been the nucleus of considerable expansion since then.

Girvan (at Girvan, 21 miles south of Ayr)
In 1962 William Grant & Sons, of Glenfiddich, built a large distilling complex costing £1,250,000 on a sixty-four acre site. As well as the grain distillery, named after the town, a

Lowland malt distillery named Ladyburn was incorporated as well. The Company thus has all the necessary resources for producing its own famed blended whisky, *Grant's Standfast*.

Moffat (3 miles east of Airdrie)

This grain distillery was built in 1964 by Inverhouse Distillers Limited with a ready water supply from the nearby Killyloch. Inverhouse Distillers Limited are a subsidiary of Publicker Industries Incorporated, Philadelphia, the distillers of 'Old Hickory', bourbon whisky. Their blend of Scotch whisky, *Inverhouse* is shipped in bulk to the United States of America.

Port Dundas (Glasgow)

A distillery was established on this site during the 18th century by Robert Macfarlane. The completion of the Forth & Clyde Canal nearby helped the distillery greatly and it remained in the Macfarlane family throughout the 19th century while developing enormously in size and output. M. Macfarlane & Company of Port Dundas distillery, were founder members of the D.C.L. in 1877 and before the end of the century it had a production capacity of $2\frac{1}{2}$ million gallons annually. It is now controlled by Scottish Grain Distillers Limited.

Strathclyde (Glasgow)

In 1927 Seager Evans, the London-Deptford based firm of gin distillers built the Strathclyde grain distillery as their first move towards entering the Scotch Whisky industry. This was to become the nucleus of a considerable distilling interest in Scotland. Their blend is marketed as *Long John*.

Tayside Region

Lochside (on the outskirts of Montrose)

In 1957, Joseph Hobbs established this distillery comprising a grain and malt distillery with a blending plant on a site formerly occupied in the 18th century by a brewery and one with ample well supplies of water. The controlling company was MacNab's Limited, and a blend was promoted called *Sandy MacNab's*. In November 1973 control passed to Destilerias Y Crianza del Whisky S.A., Madrid, Spain. They propose to discontinue the grain and blending side of the business and concentrate on the pot-still malt distilling.

One of the advertisements for *Long John* whisky

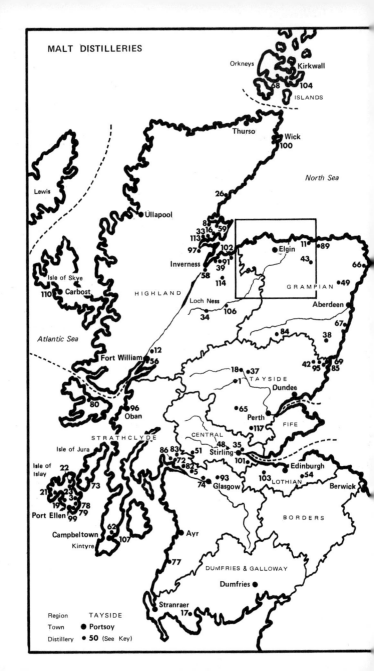

MALT DISTILLERIES

Orkneys
Kirkwall
68
104
ISLANDS

Thurso
Wick
100

North Sea

Lewis

Ullapool

26

8
3316 59
113
97
102
Elgin 11 89
43
66

Inverness
91
39
58
114

GRAMPIAN
49

Isle of Skye
110 Carbost

HIGHLAND

Loch Ness
34 106
Aberdeen

Atlantic Sea

84
38

Fort William 12
56

42 69
95 85

80

18 37
1 TAYSIDE
Dundee

96
Oban

65
Perth
117

STRATHCLYDE

Isle of Jura

CENTRAL
48 35
Stirling
101

Isle of
Islay
22

86 83
72
82
5

Edinburgh
54
103 LOTHIAN
Berwick

21
19
99
23
73
78
79

93
74 Glasgow

Port Ellen

62
Campbeltown 107
Kintyre

Ayr

BORDERS

77

DUMFRIES & GALLOWAY
Dumfries

Stranraer
17

Region   TAYSIDE
Town   ● Portsoy
Distillery   ● 50 (See Key)

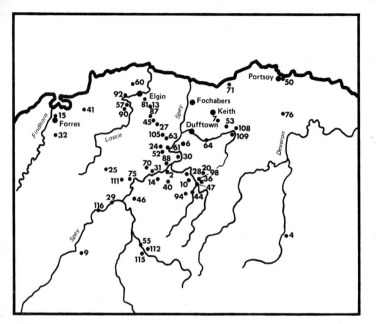

KEY

1 Aberfeldy
2 Aberlour-Glenlivet
3 Ardbeg
4 Ardmore
5 Auchentoshan
6 Auchriosk
7 Aultmore
8 Balblair
9 Balmenach
10 Balvenie
11 Banff
12 Ben Nevis
13 Ben Riach-Glenlivet
14 Benrinnes
15 Benromach-Glenlivet
16 Ben Wyvis
17 Bladnoch
18 Blair Atholl
19 Bowmore
20 Braes of Glenlivet
21 Bruichladdich
22 Bunnahabhain
23 Caol Ila
24 Caperdonich
25 Cardow
26 Clynelish
27 Coleburn
28 Convalmore
29 Cragganmore
30 Craigellachie
31 Dailuaine
32 Dallas Dhu
33 Dalmore
34 Dalwhinnie
35 Deanston
36 Dufftown-Glenlivet
37 Edradour
38 Fettercairn
39 Glen Albyn

40 Glenallachie-Glenlivet
41 Glenburgie-Glenlivet
42 Glencadam
43 Glendronach
44 Glendullan
45 Glen Elgin
46 Glenfarclas-Glenlivet
47 Glenfiddich
48 Glen Foyle
49 Glengarioch
50 Glenglassaugh
51 Glengoyne
52 Glen Grant-Glenlivet
53 Glen Keith-Glenlivet
54 Glenkinchie
55 Glenlivet, The
56 Glenlochy
57 Glenlossie
58 Glen Mhor
59 Glenmorangie
60 Glen Moray-Glenlivet
61 Glen Rothes-Glenlivet
62 Glen Scotia
63 Glen Spey
64 Glentauchers
65 Glenturret
66 Glenugie
67 Glenury-Royal
68 Highland Park
69 Hillside
70 Imperial
71 Inchgower
72 Inverleven
73 Isle of Jura
74 Kinclaith
75 Knockando
76 Knockdhu
77 Ladyburn
78 Lagavulin

79 Laphroaig
80 Ledaig
81 Linkwood
82 Littlemill
83 Loch Lomond
84 Lochnagar Royal
85 Lochside
86 Lomond
87 Longmorn-Glenlivet
88 Macallan
89 Macduff
90 Mannochmore
91 Milburn
92 Miltonduff-Glenlivet
93 Moffat
94 Mortlach
95 North Port
96 Oban
97 Ord
98 Pittyvaich-Glenlivet
99 Port Ellen
100 Pulteney
101 Rosebank
102 Royal Brackla
103 St. Magdalene
104 Scapa
105 Speyburn
106 Speyside
107 Springbank
108 Strathisla-Glenlivet
109 Strathmill
110 Talisker
111 Tamdhu-Glenlivet
112 Tamnavulin-Glenlivet
113 Teaninich
114 Tomatin
115 Tomintoul-Glenlivet
116 Tormore
117 Tullibardine

Chapter 7

The whereabouts of Malt Whisky

A glance at the map on page 52 will show that the malt distilleries are scattered over a wide area of the country. The concentration is mostly, however, in the favoured Grampian area, where conditions are ideal, between Dufftown and Elgin.

Each malt whisky differs noticeably from its neighbour and because of this individuality it is difficult to classify them accurately. A recognised classification is as follows. *Highland malts* originate north of the Highland line, which as mentioned, runs roughly from Glasgow to Dundee, and *Lowland malts* are south of this line to the border with England. *Campbeltown malts* are from the remote long peninsula running north to south to the west of Glasgow and *Island malts* originate from the islands of Skye, Islay, Jura and Orkney.

The further breakdown of some of these categories such as dividing Highland malts into Glenlivet, Dufftown and Northern malts and further sub-divisions by rivers into Deveron, Findhorn, Lossie, Nairn and Speyside malts merely tends to cause confusion. The simplest method is to deal with the malts by Regions in alphabetical order. The reader can then tell at once where each distillery is and which are to be found in each Region. An exception has been made in the case of the Islay malts, which properly belong to Strathclyde. Since they are a specific area and generally treated as one unit they have been listed under a separate heading 'Isle of Islay' at the end of the Strathclyde list of distilleries.

As with the previous chapter, the name of the distillery is shown in bold type along with the geographical location in brackets.

Central Region

Glen Foyle   (Gargunnock, 6 miles north of Stirling)
This Lowland distillery gets its water from the Campsie Fells and, according to Alfred Barnard, author of the first book on

Scotch Whisky in 1887, was 'built in 1826 by Messrs. A. Chrystal and John McNee'. It is now controlled by Brodie Hepburn Limited and the bulk of the Lowland single malt whisky distilled goes for blending.

Glengoyne   (near Killearn)

Originally known as Glenguin this (technically) Lowland malt distillery was built in 1833 at the foot of the Campsie Fells and amply supplied with water by a fifty foot fall. It is now controlled by Lang Brothers Limited, Glasgow, a subsidiary of Highland Distilleries Company Limited. The whisky distilled is a pleasant single malt from just on the imaginary 'Highland Line', bottled at 8 years and 70 degrees proof.

Rosebank   (Falkirk)

The site was originally chosen for its water supplies and, according to the Statistical Account for Scotland, the Messrs. Stark Brothers were distilling here in 1798. However, the forerunner of today's distillery complex was begun by James Rankine in 1840. In 1864 his son rebuilt the entire distillery. It is now controlled by the Distillers Agency Limited, Edinburgh, a subsidiary of the D.C.L. The whisky distilled is a light Lowland malt bottled at 70 degrees proof.

Dumfries & Galloway Region

Bladnoch   (1 mile south-east of Wigtown)

Bladnoch is the most southerly distillery in Scotland, and was built in 1817 by the McClelland family at the lower end of the village of Bladnoch from which it takes its name. It stands on the banks of the River Bladnoch and is amply supplied with water from the Carrick Hills drawn from the River Cree and the River Bladnoch. It is now controlled by the Bladnoch Distillery Limited, Glasgow, a subsidiary of Inverhouse Distillers Limited. This Lowland single malt whisky is now available bottled at 70 degrees proof.

Grampian Region

Aberlour-Glenlivet   (near the village of Aberlour)

This distillery is supplied with ample water from the Lour Burn, a tributary of the Spey. It is a good example of a

Speyside distillery in delightful surroundings beneath Ben Rinnes, not far south of Dufftown. Established in the 1860's, rebuilt in the 1880's, it is owned by the Aberlour-Glenlivet Distillery Company Limited, Aberlour. It produces a good light Speyside Highland single malt using the hyphenated Glenlivet title bottled at 8 years old and 70 degrees proof.

Ardmore   (at Kennethmont, 17 miles south of Huntly)
This malt whisky distillery was built in 1891 by William Teacher. It was modernised and enlarged in the 1950's and is still owned by William Teacher & Sons, Limited, Glasgow. The whisky distilled is entirely used for blending their noted *Highland Cream*.

Auchroisk   (near Mulben, 5 miles east of Keith)
Established in 1973, this is a new venture under the auspices of the International Distillers and Vintners, Limited. It will be interesting to sample the single malt whisky when it becomes available.

Aultmore   (near to Keith)
Established in 1896 by Alexander Edward of Forres, this distillery was sold in 1923 to John Dewar & Sons, Limited. It is now licensed to John & Robert Harvey & Company Limited, Glasgow, a subsidiary of the D.C.L. The distillery takes its peat from Forgie Moss and has excellent springs supplying ample water for its requirements. It supplies a good Speyside Highland malt whisky bottled at 12 years.

Balmanach   (3 miles north-east of Grantown-on-Spey)
James McGregor built this distillery in 1824 in the low-lying Haughs o' Cromdale and was amongst the first to be licensed after the introduction of the 1823 Act. It had ample supplies of peat from the Burnside Moss and excellent water on hand. It was famed as producing a strong tasting liqueur type of malt whisky. It is now licensed to John Crabbie & Company Limited and the entire production is used for blending purposes.

Balvenie   (close to Dufftown)
Dufftown is now rated as Scotland's whisky capital since the eclipse of Campbeltown. A local jingle runs:

> 'Rome was built on seven hills
> Dufftown stands on seven stills.'

Teachers *Highland Cream* whisky as advertised in the *Sunday Pictorial*

Balvenie was established in 1890 by William Grant on part of the land he had bought for his nearby Glenfiddich distillery. The water for distilling is taken from the fine Robbie Dubh spring and both distilleries use the nearby Fiddich Burn for cooling purposes. Still owned by the firm of William Grant & Sons, Limited, the distillery was greatly expanded in 1955. Balvenie now has its own maltings and supplies malt for Glenfiddich, and Glenfiddich has its own bottling plant and, in turn, bottles for Balvenie. The malt whisky produced is a sound Highland single malt bottled at 11 years and 100 degrees proof and tastes quite different from the neighbouring Glenfiddich.

Banff   (Mill of Banff. 1 mile from Banff)
This distillery was built in 1824 and was amongst the few distilleries bombed during the 1939–45 War. It is licensed to Slater, Rodger & Company Limited, Glasgow, a D.C.L. subsidiary and its entire production is used for blending.

Benrinnes   (on the slopes of Ben Rinnes)
In existence by 1836 and built on a site 600 feet above sea level on the slopes of Ben Rinnes (2,756 ft.) there is an ample water supply from fresh springs. It is licensed to A. & A. Crawford Limited, Leith, a subsidiary of the D.C.L. The entire output is used for blending.

Benriach-Glenlivet   (close to Elgin)
This distillery is part of the group known as The Glenlivet Distillers, Limited. Originally built in the 1890's it was wholly re-built and re-opened in 1965. The whisky produced is largely used by blenders including Hill Thomson's *Queen Anne* and *Something Special*. It is controlled by a subsidiary, the Longmorn-Glenlivet Distilleries, Limited.

Benromach   (Forres)
Built in the late boom years in 1898, this distillery is now licensed to J. & W. Hardie, Limited, a subsidiary of the D.C.L. and the entire production is used for blending.

Braes of Glenlivet   (9 miles from Dufftown)
The Braes of Glenlivet distillery is the latest to be built in Glenlivet itself. Distilling started in 1973 with three stills operating and the malt whisky produced is considered a good

Glenlivet type. The water is obtained from the hill braes above the Glen. It is intended that it will all go for blending, although in due course an 8 year old single malt may be marketed. This distillery is a subsidiary of Seagram Distillers Limited of Paisley. They are presently engaged in building another distillery, Allt-a-Bhainne, on the Dufftown–Tomintoul Road, nearer Dufftown.

Caperdonich   (Rothes)
Originally built in 1897 this distillery was linked by a pipe crossing the road with its neighbouring distillery Glen Grant at Rothes and was known then as Glen Grant No. 2. The whisky pipe remained a notable landmark for many years, although in practice only used in the first decade, since the distillery was closed in the early 1900's. Renamed Caperdonich and completely modernised and renovated it was re-opened in 1967 with a highly automated distilling plant. Control is by J. & J. Grant, Glen Grant, Limited, now part of The Glenlivet Distillers Limited.

Cardow   (Knockando, Spey Valley)
This distillery was first licensed by John Cumming on the Cardow farm and was bought by John Walker and Sons Limited in 1893 who still hold the distillers licence, as a subsidiary of the D.C.L. Its water supply is piped from the Mannoch Hill to the north-west which is 2 miles away. The distillery also gets its peat from here. It was extensively modernised in 1965 and the whisky produced is known as *Cardhu* and can be obtained bottled at 12 years and 70 degrees proof. It is considered a good Highland/Speyside malt.

Coleburn   (Elgin)
Built by John Robertson and Sons of Dundee in 1896 this small distillery's licence is held by J. & G. Stewart, a subsidiary of the D.C.L. The whisky distilled is almost all used for blending.

Convalmore   (by Dufftown)
Convalmore distillery was bought, in 1904, by W. P. Lowrie and Company Limited, now a D.C.L. subsidiary, who remain the licensed distillers. In 1910 an experimental patent-still was introduced, but it was found that the pot-still malt whisky

matured better and in 1916 the patent-still was removed. It is all used for blending.

Cragganmore   (South of Ballindalloch)
Established by John Smith in 1869 this distillery is well-sited beneath Cragganmore Hill (1,600 ft.) from which it gets its name. It is now licensed to D. & J. McCallum Limited, a D.C.L. subsidiary. Its output is used entirely for blending.

Craigellachie   (Craigellachie)
Well placed above the Spey, close to some famous salmon pools, this distillery was first built in 1890 and acquired by Mackie & Company, later to become White Horse Distillers Limited, about 10 years later. In 1927 White Horse Distillers were acquired by the D.C.L. who still retain control. The entire output is used for blending.

Dailuaine   (by Carron Burn)
Situated beneath Ben Rinnes, this distillery was built in 1852. Since 1900, it has been licensed to Dailuaine-Talisker Distilleries Limited, of which the D.C.L. obtained control in 1916. The whisky distilled is almost entirely used for blending.

Dallas Dhu   (2 miles south of Forres)
Lying in beautiful countryside this distillery was built in 1899 and was, in due course, acquired by the D.C.L. It is now licensed to Benmore Distilleries, Limited, a subsidiary of the D.C.L. and the bulk of the whisky is used for blending.

Dufftown-Glenlivet   (Dufftown)
The Dufftown-Glenlivet distillery, another using the hyphenated Glenlivet title, is situated in the Dullan Glen. Although the Dullan and Fiddich Burns flow down the Glen towards the Spey, the distillery gets its water from 'Jock's Well', which is noted for its never-failing supply of fine water. Founded in 1896 the distillery was acquired by Arthur Bell & Sons, Limited, in 1933 and is still owned by them. It produces a typical Speyside, Glenlivet or Dufftown single malt whisky, depending on which grouping is preferred. It is much used in blending, but is also bottled at 8 years old and 70 degrees proof.

Fettercairn   (6 miles south west of Stonehaven)
Close to the village of Fettercairn from which the distillery
derives its name, it was built above the river North Esk in
1824. The water supply is obtained from the Grampian
Mountains. It is now a subsidiary of the House of Fraser. The
whisky is called *Old Fettercairn* and is mostly used for
blending, although some is available in bottle.

Glenallachie   (Aberlour)
A modern distillery built in 1968 by Mackinlay-McPherson
Limited, a subsidiary of Scottish & Newcastle Breweries.

Glenburgie-Glenlivet and Glencraig   (near Forres)
It is said that this distillery was established in 1810 by the Paul
family. It was subsequently acquired by the firm of James &
George Stodart, Limited, Dumbarton, who were themselves
taken over by Hiram Walker (Scotland) Limited, in 1930.
The distillery is still controlled by J. & G. Stodart, Limited
and it is notable that although 20 miles from Glenlivet, the
firm finds the use of the hyphenated Glenlivet fully justified.
The whisky distilled is a good Highland malt. The Glencraig
distillery is part of the complex.

Glendronach   (near Huntly)
The Glendronach distillery lying in the Forgue valley on the
Dronach burn was built in 1826 by James Allardyce. It used to
add the hyphenated Glenlivet to its name, but since being
acquired by William Teacher & Sons, Limited, in the early
1960's and being considerably enlarged, this has been
dropped. Local control is in the hands of Glendronach
Distillery Company, Limited, Huntly. Once noted as
producing a malt whisky tasting like a liqueur, most was used
for blending until recently. Glendronach malt whisky is now
available at 70 degrees proof.

Glendullan   (Dufftown)
Another of the Dufftown distilleries, it was built by William
Williams & Sons, Limited, of Aberdeen and is now controlled
by Macdonald Greenlees, Limited, a subsidiary of the D.C.L.
At one time it used the hyphenated Glenlivet addition to its
name, being known as Glendullan-Glenlivet, but this has now
been dropped. Just the same, as might be expected, the
distillery produces a good Highland single malt whisky much

of which goes for blending, but some of which is bottled at 12 years old and 70 degrees proof.

Glen Elgin   (Glen Elgin)
Established in 1898 by Peter Mackie, subsequently the highly individualistic Director of White Horse Distillers, it gets its water supplies from springs in Glen Rothes. At one time the distillery used the hyphenated Glenlivet addition. It was acquired by the Scottish Malt Distillers in 1936, but it is still controlled by White Horse Distillers Limited, a D.C.L. subsidiary. The entire output is used for blending.

Glenfarclas-Glenlivet   (above Ballindalloch)
The Glenfarclas-Glenlivet distillery still proudly uses the hyphenated Glenlivet title. It stands exposed to the elements on the bare moorland, where the river Avon joins the Spey, a little way off the main road to Elgin. Both water and peat are readily available to hand. The distillery was founded in 1836 by Robert Hay, on whose death in 1865 it was acquired by J. & G. Grant Limited. It is still owned by the family firm and a descendant, George Grant, is still Managing Director. The single malt whisky is bottled at 8 years and at 70, 100 and 105 degrees proof, also at 12 years at 70 degrees proof. The distillery has been awarded the Gold Seal in London by Club Oenologigue, three years running, for fifteen years old 80 degrees Glenfarclas.

The distillery provides every facility for visitors, including a well laid out museum with examples of illicit stills and full explanations of the distilling processes amongst other attractions. Eight years old 80 degrees proof are bottled and sold to distillery visitors. It is on the 'Whisky Trail' organised by the local Tourist Authority which consists of a route through delightful countryside round distilleries open to visitors. (Further details from the Grampian Tourist Authority, Elgin. Telephone: Elgin 2666.)

Glenfiddich   (Dufftown)
Glenfiddich, is perhaps the best-known Dufftown distillery today, and has an interesting background. It was established by William Grant, who, after twenty years' experience in the neighbouring distillery of Mortlach, bought the land on the Fiddich Burn. He bought the plant from the disused Cardow

distillery for £120 and set about building his own distillery with the assistance of his five sons. He used the water from the Fiddich Burn for cooling purposes and the water from the Robbie Dubh Spring for distillation, on the lines of the Belvenie distillery. He started distilling in 1887 and the venture prospered immediately. One of his sons established the Glendronach distillery. In 1955, the distillery, still controlled by William Grant & Sons, Limited, expanded greatly, along with Balvenie. Whereas Balvenie now has its own maltings and supplies both distilleries with malt, Glenfiddich is the only distillery apart from Springbank to have its own bottling plant, and bottles the product of both distilleries. The triangular bottle and the *Glenfiddich Pure Malt Whisky* which is bottled at 8 and 10 years at 70 degrees proof are both well known.

The original building has now been turned into a museum and tourist centre, where visitors are welcome—some 56,000 in 1972 and all offered a dram! This is another distillery on the 'Whisky Trail' promoted by the local Tourist Authority.

Glengarioch   (Old Meldrum Village)
Not far from Meldrum House, this distillery was, reputedly, first built in the 1790's. It was bought by J. F. Thomson of Leith in 1840 and in the mid-1880's was acquired by William Sanderson blender of the famed *Vat 69*. Later, due to lack of water, the distillery was closed in 1968. It was acquired in 1970 by Stanley P. Morrison, Limited (Whisky Brokers), of Glasgow who re-started distilling when a deep well was sunk. Half a million gallons were distilled in 1973 and this single malt Highland whisky is available in bottle at over 8 years and 70 degrees proof.

Visitors are welcome, at any time except for three weeks in July.

Glenglassaugh   (2 miles inland from Portsoy)
This distillery was built in 1875 with water supplies from the river Glassaugh and the Knock hills. It is owned today by the Highland Distilleries Limited and, in 1964, was almost entirely rebuilt, so that it is now one of the more modern distilleries in Scotland. The whisky is used almost entirely for blending.

Glen Keith-Glenlivet   (Keith)

This distillery was built by Chivas Brothers in 1958 on a site across the small Isla River from the other Chivas distilleries known as Strathisla-Glenlivet. One of the latest distilleries to adopt the hyphenated Glenlivet title, the entire production is used for blending.

Glentauchers   (4½ miles west of Keith)

Founded in 1898 by the Glentauchers Distillery Company Limited, the distillery was acquired by James Buchanan and Company Limited in 1906. They still hold the licence, although they are now part of the D.C.L. complex. The entire output is used for blending.

Glen Grant-Glenlivet   (Rothes)

James & John Grant had been distilling at nearby Dandaleith since 1834 before establishing this distillery in 1840. By 1865 they had become sufficiently successful to warrant modernising and enlarging the distillery. In 1897 they established Caperdonich, called at that time Glen Grant No. 2, on the other side of the road. In 1901, however, this second venture was closed, only to be re-opened again in 1967. The parent company is now The Glenlivet Distillers Limited, but Glen Grant is still controlled by J. & J. Grant, Glen Grant, Limited and the whisky is available in bottles at 5, 10 and 15 years and 70 degrees proof. It is amongst the finest Speyside/Glenlivet single malt whiskies.

The Glenlivet (between Tomintoul and Ballindalloch)

The history of The Glenlivet has been outlined on pages 33–34 from the first licence taken out in 1824, to the present day. Lying in the hollow of Glenlivet, with the hill rising all round, the distillery has ample supplies of peat from Faemussach moss and water from the nearby Josie's well. Throughout the slump years after the 1914–18 War, The Glenlivet Distillery was still producing whisky when every other distillery in Scotland had ceased production. Demand for The Glenlivet whisky has not ceased since the days when it was recognised by George IV as one of the finest whiskies in Scotland. Two local jingles highlight the fame of The Glenlivet. The first mentions the local castles:

> 'Glenlivet has its castles three
> Drumin, Blairfindy and Deskie,
> And also one distillery
> More famous than the castles three.'

The second, the old Distilleries:

> 'Auchorachan, Upper Drumin and Minmore,
> Those were the distilleries of yore,
> Which made Glenlivet whisky famed
> And ever The Glenlivet named.'

They merged in 1952 with J. & J. Grant, Glen-Grant Limited, another fine firm of malt whisky distillers, but the individual whiskies remained unaltered. The Glenlivet Distillers, Limited, now control the overall group, to which Hill Thomson & Company Limited and Longmorn-Glenlivet, were joined in 1970. George & J. G. Smith continue to produce a fine 12 year old malt whisky, The Glenlivet, at 70 degrees proof. It remains amongst the finest.

Glenlossie   (3½ miles south-west of Elgin)
This distillery was built not far from the River Lossie, by John Duff & Company Limited of Elgin in 1876. It is now licensed to John Haig & Company Limited, a subsidiary of the D.C.L., and the entire production is used for blending.

Glen Moray-Glenlivet   (near Elgin)
Established in 1893, this distillery is another which has found it worth while to maintain the hyphenated Glenlivet addition to its name. It is controlled by Macdonald & Muir Limited and the whisky is a typical Speyside/Glenlivet single malt mostly used for blending.

Glenrothes-Glenlivet   (Rothes)
Built in 1878 this distillery was backed, initially, by a syndicate of local Speyside businessmen, including the Provost of Rothes, Robert Dick. It was acquired by the Highland Distilleries Company Limited which was formed in 1887 and is still controlled by them. The distillery produces a fine Highland/Speyside/Glenlivet single malt whisky bottled at 8, 10 and 20 years at 80 degrees proof.

Glenury Royal   (near Stonehaven)
In 1836, Captain Barclay Allardice of Urie established this
distillery on the edge of the Cowie Burn. It runs through Glen
Urie and provides a source of good pure water. Acquired in
due course by D.C.L. the distillery is now licensed to John
Gilton & Company Limited. The whisky is mostly used in
blending, although some of this Highland single malt is
available in the bottle at 70 degrees proof.

Glen Spey   (Rothes)
A local grain merchant, James Stewart established this
distillery in 1885. It was purchased in 1887 by the enterprising
firm of W. & A. Gilbey, who saw that the *Phylloxera* disease
was adversely affecting the wine trade in France and that
there was a future for Scotch Whisky. In 1962, along with
Gilbey Twiss, Justerini & Brooks and United Vintners, they
formed a new group called International Distillers &
Vintners, Limited. The distillery is still controlled by W. &
A. Gilbey, Limited, and most of the whisky produced is used
for blending.

Glenugie   (Peterhead)
This is the most easterly distillery in Scotland, situated close to
the North Sea, and established in 1875. The sandy countryside
of the district around it provides both barley and soft water.
Since 1937 it has been owned by Long John International,
U.S.A. The malt whisky produced is used entirely for
blending.

Imperial   (at Carron in Strathspey)
This distillery was established in 1887 by Thomas Mackenzie
who already owned Dailuaine and the Talisker Distilleries.
He incorporated all three properties in 1898 as the Dailuaine-
Talisker Distilleries Limited. Modernised in 1955–56 when an
electric distilling plant was installed, it is one one of the well
known Speyside distilleries. It is still licensed to Dailuaine-
Talisker Distilleries Limited, a subsidiary of the D.C.L. and
most of the whisky distilled is used for blending.

Inchgower   (at Rathven, near Fochabers)
Originally established around 1824 by Alexander Wilson
close to Cullen, this distillery was moved to Rathven, in 1871.
This was because there was a ready supply of water from the

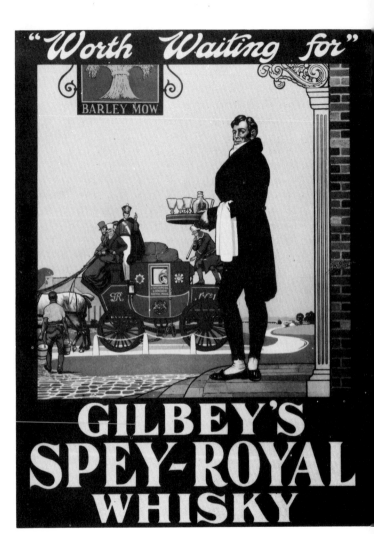

One of Gilbey's advertisements for their *Spey-Royal* whisky

Letter Burn and the springs at Aultmoor. The distillery was acquired by Arthur Bell & Sons, Limited in 1936. It has been considerably modernised and its whisky is almost entirely used for blending.

Knockando (Knockando)

This distillery was built by Ian Thomson in 1898 at the end of the whisky boom in a good position above the Spey. It is now controlled by Justerini & Brooks, a subsidiary of International Distillers & Vintners. The Speyside single malt whisky distilled is principally used for blending.

Knockdhu (at Grange, 4 miles east of Keith)

This distillery lies above the small river Isla, from which it draws its water supplies. It dates from 1893 and was the first malt whisky distillery to be built by the D.C.L. It is now licensed to the firm of James Munro & Son, Limited, a subsidiary of the D.C.L. and the entire production is used for blending.

Linkwood (1 mile south-east of Elgin)

This small distillery was built by William Brown in 1821. It was re-built in 1873 and modernised in the 1960's. The licence is held by John McEwan and Company Limited, a D.C.L. subsidiary. The whisky distilled is bottled at 12 years and 70 degrees proof and, though not well known, is highly regarded.

Longmorn-Glenlivet ($2\frac{1}{2}$ miles south of Elgin)

Near the village of Longmorn, this distillery is particularly worth noting. The water supply is from a never-failing local spring and the peat is obtained from Mannoch Hill in the background. Proudly using the hyphenated Glenlivet addition to its name, this distillery is controlled by the Longmorn-Glenlivet Distilleries, Limited, a subsidiary of The Glenlivet Distillers, Limited. The whisky distilled is amongst the finest Speyside/Glenlivet single malts, bottled at 10 years and 70 degrees proof. Some regard it as after dinner whisky, others may prefer it before a meal. It has been suggested that blended in suitable proportions with The Glenlivet, Glen Grant and possibly Macallan and Clynelish, there can be no better drink. Finding the right proportions, however, would no doubt be an interesting task in itself!

Macallan   (Craigellachie)

The distillery was built in 1824 on Macallan's farm above a ford over the Spey which the cattle drovers used on their way south. It passed through several hands before being bought in 1892 by Roderick Kemp, who greatly enlarged it. In 1946 the private company R. Kemp, Macallan-Glenlivet Limited was formed. In 1965 the distillery was doubled in size due to steadily increasing demand and it is significant that it was the first to drop the hyphenated Glenlivet addition to its name. The distillery is still run by descendants of Roderick Kemp and it has been decided never to sell the whisky under 10 years old. It is undoubtedly among the best malt whiskies available today at 10 and 15 years and 70, 80 and 100 degrees proof.

Macduff   (near Banff)

The Macduff distillery was built in 1960 by Brodie-Hepburn, Limited, and is one of the very few distilleries which produces a whisky with a different name to its own. The whisky is known as *Glendeveron* after the nearby river Deveron, which supplies water for cooling purposes. It is bottled as single malt whisky at 5 years old and 75 degrees proof by William Lawson Distillers Limited, Coatbridge.

Mannochmore   ($3\frac{1}{2}$ miles south of Elgin)

Opened in 1972 and close to the River Lossie, Mannochmore distillery is licensed to John Haig and Company Limited, a subsidiary of the D.C.L. and the entire production is used for blending.

Miltonduff-Glenlivet and Mosstowie   (just south of Elgin)

Close to the famed Pluscarden Priory ruins, this distillery was founded in 1824. The old mash house of the distillery is said to have been built on the site of the priory brewhouse. The water of the Black Burn flowing from the peaty slopes of the Black Hill provides an ample water supply. The distillery is now controlled by a subsidiary, George Ballantine & Sons, of Dumbarton. The Mosstowie distillery is part of the same complex. Although twenty miles from Glenlivet the use of the hyphenated addition to the name defines accurately that this is another very sound Speyside/Glenlivet single malt whisky. It is bottled at 13 years and 85 degrees proof.

Mortlach (Dufftown)

This distillery was first licensed in 1824 by James Findlater. Built in a hollow in the hills just outside Dufftown on the River Dullan it draws its water from a locally-famed Priest's well. It is now controlled by George Cowie and Son Limited, a D.C.L. subsidiary. Although it has dropped the hyphenated Glenlivet title, by which it was always known, the distillery produces a good Dufftown/Glenlivet/Speyside single malt whisky. It is available in bottle and is notably different from others produced around Dufftown.

Pittyvaich-Glenlivet (Dufftown)

Close to the sister distillery of Dufftown-Glenlivet, this distillery was first established in 1973 and started operating in 1974. An addition to Arthur Bell and Sons Distilleries, the whisky will principally be used for blending.

Royal Lochnagar (1 mile from Balmoral)

This distillery stands on the lower slopes of the Lochnagar Mountain (3,768 ft.) and was established by John Robertson, a noted illicit distiller in his day, and was acquired by John Begg in 1845. It was after a visit by Queen Victoria and Prince Albert in 1845, that the addition of the prefix 'Royal' was permitted. It is now licensed to John Begg, Limited, a subsidiary of the D.C.L. and the whisky is used for blending.

Speyburn (Rothes)

Built for John Hopkins and Company Limited in 1897, this distillery used to use the hyphenated Glenlivet addition to its name. It is now licensed to John Robertson and Son, Perth, a D.C.L. subsidiary. The entire output is used for blending.

Strathisla-Glenlivet (Keith)

Originally named the Milton Distillery, this distillery was founded in 1786 by George Taylor. It was ultimately purchased by Chivas Brothers, Limited, themselves a subsidiary of Joseph Seagrams Limited, Canada, in 1950. The name was changed to Strathisla, and, at the same time, the hyphenated Glenlivet added, although some considerable distance from the Livet. The distillery, in fact, obtains its water for cooling from the River Isla, and water for distilling is obtained from a reservoir filled by a spring in the hills. On the other side of the River Isla stands the sister distillery, Glen Keith-Glenlivet which was built in 1956 and provides malt for Strathisla. The single malt whisky produced is not all used for blending the noted *Chivas Regal* and some is bottled. It is a full-bodied Dufftown/Glenlivet/Speyside type.

Strathmill   (Keith)

Originally called the Glenisla-Glenlivet Distillery, Strathmill was built on the site of a former mill in 1891 and acquired by W. & A. Gilbey in 1895. Initially, they marketed malt whisky only, but then turned to blending and produced their noted *Glen Spey*. In 1962 they merged with Gilbey Twiss, Justerini & Brooks and United Vintners to form International Distillers & Vintners Limited. The output is used for blending.

Tamdhu-Glenlivet   (in the Parish of Knockando)

This distillery built in 1897 on the banks of the Spey is now owned by the Highland Distilleries Company Limited. The position of the distillery and the use of the hyphenated Glenlivet addition to the name indicates that this is a good, slightly peaty, Speyside/Glenlivet single malt whisky. It is very popular abroad and, unfortunately, hard to find in this country, but worth the effort.

Tamnavulin-Glenlivet   (Tomnavoulin)

Built in 1965 in the hills on the west bank of the River Livet, using water from a burn running into it, this can be described as a typical Speyside/Glenlivet distillery and, by position alone, the hyphenated Glenlivet is justified. Controlled by Tamnavulin-Glenlivet Distillery Company Limited, it is a subsidiary of Invergordon Distillers, Limited. The single malt Speyside-Glenlivet whisky may be obtained in bottle at 75 degrees proof.

Tomintoul-Glenlivet   (Tomintoul)

The Tomintoul-Glenlivet Distillery Company Limited established this distillery in 1965, in Tomintoul the highest village in Scotland. At over 1,100 feet above sea level the distillery is the highest in the Region. Water is amply supplied by the Ballantuan spring close to the distillery. The distillery is still controlled by the Tomintoul-Glenlivet Distillery Company Limited, a subsidiary of the House of Fraser.

Tormore   (Advie, 7 miles north of Grantown-on-Spey)
Built by Seager Evans & Company between 1958 and 1960, this was the first distillery to be built on Speyside this century. It was a complete breakaway from traditional designs, and consists of a distillery, warehouses and cooperage, as well as houses for the distillery workers built in Kemnay granite. Ample water supplies are available from the nearby Loch an Oir (Gaelic for Lake of Gold). Now part of Long John International, much of the whisky distilled here is used for blending, but some *Tormore* is bottled as a good 10 year old single malt and sold through Seager Evans & Company Limited, Westminster, London.

Highland Region

Balblair   (5 miles north-west of Tain)
Balblair distillery dates back to the days of illicit distilling in the 18th century. The position is ideal with ample water supplies and in an area known as 'the parish of peats'. The distillery was greatly enlarged by Andrew Ross & Son, in 1872. Now controlled by the Balblair Distillery Company Limited, a subsidiary of Hiram Walker & Sons (Scotland) Limited, it distils a pleasant single malt whisky.

Ben Nevis   (north of Fort William)
At the foot of Ben Nevis (4,406 ft.) this distillery, taking its name from the highest mountain in Britain, has one of the finest positions with ample water and peat supplies. It was founded in 1825, as the first legal distillery in the Lochaber area, by John McDonald, who was known far and wide as 'Long John'. His son Donald P. McDonald built the pier on Loch Linnhe to ship his whisky south. Control is now in the hands of the Ben Nevis Distillery (Fort William) Limited, and the entire production is used for blending.

Ben Wyvis   (between Dingwall and Strathpeffer)
Positioned beneath Ben Wyvis (3,429 ft.), the distillery gets its water from Loch Ussie over three miles away. It dates back to the 1880's and is owned by Invergordon Distillers, Limited. The single malt whisky distilled is used entirely for blending.

Clynelish (1 mile inland from Brora)

This distillery was established in 1819 to provide a market for the grain produced by Highlanders from their coastal allotments after the notorious 'Clearances' in the early 19th century. During these, many Highlanders were evicted from their inland homes by the landowners, and were forced to settle on the coast. The distillery is now licensed to Ainstie and Heilbron (Distillers) Limited, Glasgow, a D.C.L. subsidiary. The Highland single malt whisky distilled has long been placed amongst the best. It is available bottled at 12 years and 70 and 80 degrees proof, also at 15 years and 90 degrees proof.

Dalmore (on the River Alness)

This distillery was built in 1839 above the Cromarty Firth and overlooking the Black Isle. In 1867 it was acquired by Mackenzie Brothers, who merged with Whyte & Mackay in 1960. It is now controlled by Mackenzie Brothers, Dalmore, Limited, a subsidiary of the House of Fraser. A lot of the Highland single malt whisky distilled is used for blending Whyte & Mackay's *Special*, or *Supreme*, or *21 Years Old*, it is also available bottled at 12 and 20 years and 70 or 75 degrees proof.

Dalwhinnie (midway between Perth and Inverness)

Sited in the Pass of Drumochter, this distillery was built in 1898 at a height of 1,174 feet. It was, then, indisputably the highest distillery in Scotland although this is now claimed by the Tomintoul-Glenlivet Distillery in the Grampian Region. It is now licensed to James Buchanan & Company Limited, a subsidiary of the D.C.L. The entire production is used for blending.

Glen Albyn (Inverness)

Provost Sutherland of Inverness established this distillery in 1846, but in the 1860's it was turned into a flour mill. In 1884, however, it was re-built and re-sited alongside the Caledonian Canal basin. It is now operated by Scottish Malt Distillers, a subsidiary of the D.C.L., and the entire production is used for blending.

Glenlochy (north of Fort William)

Situated close to Loch Lochy at the start of the Caledonian

Canal this distillery was established in 1898 by David McAndie of Nairn, and is sited in superb countryside. It is now operated by Scottish Malt Distillers, a subsidiary of the D.C.L. and the entire production is used for blending.

Glen Mohr   (Inverness)

Sited only about a hundred yards from the Glen Albyn distillery, Glen Mohr was built in 1892 by John Birnie an ex-Provost of Inverness in partnership with James Mackinlay. Although it uses the same water and peat as its neighbouring distillery, the whiskies are quite distinctive. It is controlled now by Mackinlays and Birnie Limited, a subsidiary of D.C.L. Although much is used for blending purposes, it is available bottled at 10 years and 70 degrees proof.

Glenmorangie   (1 mile west of Tain)

Originally a brewery in the early 18th century, it was not until 1843 that the distillery was built in this splendid position overlooking the Dornoch Firth. Water is supplied by the springs in Torlogie Hill, but although available locally, it has been found simpler to get peat from the Aberdeen area. The distillery was acquired in 1918 by Macdonald and Muir, Limited, Leith. The whisky distilled in this distillery is a very fine distinctive single malt which must be amongst the best.

Milburn   (Inverness)

Established in 1807, this distillery was acquired in 1892 by two brothers, members of the Haig family. The licence is now in the hands of Macleay Duff (Distillers) Limited, Glasgow, another D.C.L. subsidiary. The entire production is used for blending.

Ord   (Muir of Ord, 3 miles north of Beauly)

This distillery was established in 1838 and is now licensed to Peter Dawson Limited, Glasgow, a subsidiary of the D.C.L. Ample water supplies are available from Glen Oran and Oran Burn and the area was famous for illicit distilling even as late as the end of the 19th century. The distillery is notable for mixing heather with the peat in the malt drying process, and the whisky, bottled at 75 degrees proof, is regarded as amongst the finest Highland single malts.

Pulteney (near Wick)

The distillery was established in 1826 by James Henderson. It is situated near the ruined castle, the Auld Man of Wick. There are ample water supplies available, including the Loch of Hempriggs, and peat is no problem in a countryside where the houses are often roofed with it. The lack of good and easy communications in this area is shown by the fact that this is the only distillery in the Caithness District and the furthest north of all mainland distilleries. It was closed during the post-war whisky slump in the 1920's and only re-opened in 1951. The distillery is now controlled by James & George Stodart Limited, Dumbarton, since 1955 a subsidiary of Hiram Walker & Sons, Limited. The whisky produced is known as *Old Pulteney* and has a distinctive flavour of its own. It is also reputedly amongst the fastest maturing of malt whiskies.

Royal Brackla (3½ miles south-west of Nairn)

The Royal Brackla distillery was founded by Captain William Fraser in 1812 and obtained the 'Royal' prefix because William IV ordered its whisky. It was acquired by John Bisset and Company Limited, in 1926 who are still the licence holders although a subsidiary now of the D.C.L. The bulk of the single malt whisky is used for blending.

Speyside (4 miles south of Kingussie)

Situated on the banks of the River Trowie, this distillery was only completed in 1974, close to the site of an old 19th century distillery. It is controlled by the Speyside Distillery Company Limited and is another distilling venture by the Christie family who established the North of Scotland grain distillery.

Talisker (Carbost, Isle of Skye)

Established in 1843, the Talisker Distillery is on the Isle of Skye. It is now controlled by the Dailuaine-Talisker Distilleries, a D.C.L. subsidiary. The barley and malt are obtained from the mainland. Water is supplied by the nearby Carbost Burn. The whisky has its own distinctive flavour, quite different from the Islay malts, but outstandingly a west coast malt. It is obtainable in bottle at 70, 80, and 100 degrees proof.

Teananich   (on the banks of the River Alness)
First built by Captain H. Munro in 1800, this distillery was the only one in the area to survive the taxation of the period. It is now owned by R. H. Thompson & Company (Distillers) Limited, a subsidiary of the D.C.L. The entire production is used for blending.

Tomatin   (12 miles south of Inverness)
Built at a height of over 1,000 feet in the Monadhliath mountains, this distillery occasionally suffers from a water shortage in a dry year. It claims very ancient origins, but dates effectually from 1909 when it was entirely re-built and modernised. Since then it has remained well to the fore in mechanisation and its production is the largest of any single malt distillery, at over 2,000,000 gallons a year. Owned by the Tomatin Distillers, Limited it produces a good peaty malt whisky which is much admired.

Islands Authorities

Highland Park   (Kirkwall)
This distillery was built on the hill overlooking Kirkwall, on the site of the bothy of a famous illicit distiller named Magnus Eunson. Eunson was a Church officer, and an unmitigated rogue, who constantly evaded being caught with his illicit whisky by hiding it under the pulpit, or by similar stratagems. The 'legal' distillery is said to have been established in 1789 by David Robertson, and was acquired in 1895 by the Grant family. It is still controlled by James Grant & Company Limited, who since 1936 have been owned by Highland Distilleries, Limited. The distillery has its own maltings, though barley has to be imported from the mainland. The water supply comes from two local wells. The Orkney peat used has a distinctive aroma and the whisky has a special characteristic flavour, aided by the peat and the small quantity of heather which is burnt with it. The single malt whisky is bottled at from 70 to 100 degrees proof and the stronger quality has been likened to a fine brandy.

Scapa   (Kirkwall)
Scapa distillery, the only other in Kirkwall and Orkney, overlooks Scapa Bay. It takes its water from the Lingrow

Burn and local springs. It was built in 1885 by Macfarlane & Townsend, and is now controlled by a subsidiary, Taylor & Ferguson Limited. The entire malt whisky production is used for blending.

Lothian Region

Glenkinchie   (close to Pencaitland)
Situated in the Kinchie Glen through which the Kinchie Burn flows to the River Tyne, this distillery was established around 1840 by James Gray, a local farmer. It is now licensed to John Haig and Company Limited, a subsidiary of the D.C.L. A Lowland single malt whisky is produced which is ideal for blending.

St. Magdalene   (Linlithgow)
Built on the lands of St. Mary's Cross in the late 18th century by Sebastian Henderson, this distillery had to compete, in the 19th century, with as many as five other distilleries in the town. It is the only surviving distillery and is licensed to John Hopkins and Company Limited, a D.C.L. subsidiary. The entire whisky production is used for blending.

Strathclyde Region

Auchentoshan   (close to the Erskine Bridge)
Established in 1825 on the road from Glasgow to Dumbarton and near to what is said to have been St. Patrick's birthplace. It lies just below the 'Highland Line' so the whisky is called a Lowland malt, although peat and water are obtained from north of the 'Highland Line', the latter, from Loch Cochno in the Kilpatrick Hills. The distilling process is unusual in that three stills are used instead of the usual two. The distillery is owned by Eadie Cairns Limited, Glasgow and the whisky is available in bottle at 5 years and 70 degrees proof, from their off-licence in Hope Street, Glasgow. They also have a well-known blend, *Cairns*.

Glen Scotia   (Campbeltown)
The distillery was first named the Scotia, and built by the Galbraith family in 1832, close to the Parliament Square in the centre of Campbeltown. With ample water, peat, coal and barley available locally during the 19th century it was one of

the thirty-four distilleries which provided this small town with the proud boast that it was 'the whisky capital of Scotland'. Indifferent distilling and the sale of immature whiskies gave the area a bad name with disastrous results. The Glen Scotia distillery is now one of the only two left. Its present owners, are A. Gillies & Company Limited, Newton Place, Glasgow. The whisky has a rich, peaty, slightly oily taste with an affinity to Irish whiskey. It can be obtained in bottle from the proprietors in Glasgow, or locally.

Inverleven (Dumbarton)

Hiram Walker and Sons (Scotland) Limited established this distillery in 1938 and, technically, it is situated right on the 'Highland Line'. It is usually classed as a Lowland malt distillery. It gets its water from the River Leven and Lochs Lomond and Humphrey. The output is used entirely for blending.

Visitors are welcome.

Isle of Jura (Isle of Jura)

The distillery was first built in 1810 and re-built in 1963 by Charles Mackinlay & Company Limited, a subsidiary of Scottish & Newcastle Breweries, after being closed for about 50 years. Control is in the hands of another subsidiary, Isle of Jura Distillery Company Limited, of Craighouse. The whisky first became available in 1973 as a single malt with a distinctive west coast flavour.

Kinclaith (near Glasgow)

This distillery was built in 1957 and is controlled by Long John Distilleries, Limited, Glasgow. The entire production is used for blending.

Ladyburn (Girvan)

This Lowland malt distillery built in 1962 is part of the distilling complex of William Grant & Sons. The bulk of the single malt whisky distilled is used for blending in the famous *Grant's Standfast*.

Moffat (Airdrie)

Built during the 1960's by Inver House Distillers Limited, this forms part of their whisky distilling complex. See entry under Moffat, page 50, chapter 6. There is a pot-still malt whisky distillery providing a Lowland malt called *Glenflagler*.

Ledaig (Tobermory, Isle of Mull)

This distillery, originally called the Tobermory Distillery was built in 1823 and owned by the Mackill Brothers who were local farmers. Production ceased in the 1920's and the Ledaig Distillery (Tobermory) Limited has recently re-formed and the distillery re-started.

It will be interesting to see how this compares with the other island malts when the whisky becomes available.

Littlemill (Bowling, 12 miles from Glasgow)

A distillery was first established in the late part of the 18th century, but the present site probably dates from around 1800. It is now owned by Barton Distilling (Scotland) Limited, Alexandria, and, although it uses Highland peat and water from the Kilpatrick Hills it is classified as a Lowland malt distillery. The whisky produced is used for blending, but can be bought bottled at 75 degrees proof.

Loch Lomond (Alexandria)

This is another distillery owned by Barton Distilling (Scotland) Limited and is sited on an old printing and bleach works. It is also sited on the 'Highland Line' and just qualiifies as producing a Highland malt whisky. It is mostly used for blending, but some can be bought bottled at 70 degrees proof.

Lomond (Dumbarton)

This distillery should not be confused with the Loch Lomond distillery. It is owned by Hiram Walker and Sons (Scotland) Limited and works in conjunction with their complex at Dumbarton. A unique facet of the distilling here is a straight sided still invented by Fred Whiting. The whisky is mostly used for blending.

Oban (Oban)

Established in 1794 by the Stevenson family, this distillery was part of the development carried out by the family who were responsible for making Oban a thriving centre. The water supply comes from two lochs in Ardconnel a mile above Oban in the peaty uplands. It is now licensed to William Greer and Company Limited, a subsidiary of the D.C.L., after changing hands several times. It was closed in 1968 but re-opened again in 1969. When available, the whisky should be an interesting single malt.

Springbank (Campbeltown)

The only Campbeltown distillery to survive without closing, Springbank, was established by the Mitchell family in the late 1820's and is still owned by J. & A. Mitchell & Company Limited, the family company. An unusual feature is that a special spirit still is used for foreshots and feints, instead of being returned for re-distillation as is usually the case. This may contribute to the notable lightness and mellowness of the whisky which has been compared to a Lowland malt. It has three times won the championship award at the Wine & Spirit Fair at Ljubljana in Yugoslavia. Available in limited quantities only at 80 degrees proof and twelve years old it is clearly a noteworthy whisky.

Isle of Islay

Although the Isle of Islay is part of the Strathclyde Region, the Islay malts are quite distinctive and better dealt with as a group, as follows.

Ardbeg (south-east coast)

Sited close to the sea, this distillery was established by the McDougall family around 1815. It is now owned by the Ardbeg Distillery Limited, one of the last independent distilleries in Islay. Lochs Uigeadale and Arinambeast provide the water supply and together with the local peat produce a notable Islay malt. Although the bulk of the Islay malts are used for blending and, indeed, few blends are without them, the whisky produced at Ardbeg can be bought in the bottle at 8 years old, and is obtainable through the Ardbeg Distillery Limited, West George Street, Glasgow.

Bowmore (beside the River Laggan)

This is another typical Islay distillery sited almost on the sea and was acquired by Sherriff's Bowmore Distillery Limited in association with Stanley P. Morrison of Glasgow in 1963. A fine water supply is readily available from the River Laggan and this above standard Islay malt may be obtained bottled at 8 years and 70 degrees proof from Morrison's of Glasgow.

Bruichladdich   (on Lochindaal)

Built in 1881, this is another Islay distillery which is sited directly by the sea. It is controlled, today, by the Bruichladdich Distillery Company Limited, now a subsidiary of the Invergordon Distillers Limited. Its water supplies are obtained from an inland reservoir which may be why the whisky lacks the slightly medicinal taste often associated with Islay malts. There is some debate as to how this flavour is found in most of the whiskies produced in Islay and it is sometimes thought to come from the seaweed in the peat. It is significant, however, that the whisky produced at Bruichladdich, although using the same peat, does not have this particular trait and the main difference is in its water supplies. Although used mainly for blending, the whisky is available bottled at 75 degrees proof and is a good example of a rich Islay malt.

Bunnahabhain   (on the north-east coast)

This distillery is now controlled by the Highland Distilleries Company Limited and the whisky is used entirely for blending.

Caol Ila   (north of Port Askaig)

Built in 1846 and overlooking the Sound of Jura the Caol Ila Distillery gets its water supplies from Loch Torrabus—said to be the finest on Islay. It has its own private wharf through which it gets its supplies of barley and ships its whisky in return. The distillery is now controlled by Bulloch, Lade and Company Limited, subsidiaries of the D.C.L. Most of the whisky is used for blending but a quantity is exported under the name *Glen Isla*. At present, none is available in the home market.

Lagavulin   (Lagavulin, east of Port Ellen)

There is considerable argument as to which is the oldest distillery in Islay since the island was the scene of much illicit distilling, but Lagavulin probably dates back as far as any. It is built beside the village of Lagavulin in a small bay and obtains its water from lochs in the hill of Solan. Peter Mackie learned his distilling at Lagavulin and used it as the basis for his famous *White Horse* blend. When White Horse Distillers were taken over by the D.C.L. in 1927 they also acquired this

New pot-stills at the Caol Ila Distillery, Isle of Islay ➤

Islay malt distillery. The distillers licence is still in the hands of White Horse Distillers, Limited, Glasgow, and the bulk of the whisky goes to the blenders, but some is available bottled at 75 degrees proof.

Laphroaig   (1 mile from Port Ellen)
Situated on the shore, this distillery was built in 1820 by the Johnston family, who were local farmers. It is now controlled by D. Johnston and Company (Laphroaig) Limited, a subsidiary of Long John Distilleries Limited. Much of the whisky goes to make the notable blend *Islay Mist* which is available locally and from Seager Evans and Company Limited, Queen Anne's Gate, Westminster, London, bottled at 10 years and 75 degrees proof.

Port Ellen   ($\frac{1}{2}$ mile from Port Ellen)
This distillery was established in 1825 and although closed in 1930 was re-opened in 1967 after being modernised and enlarged. It is now licensed to Low, Robertson and Company, a subsidiary of the D.C.L.

Tayside Region

Aberfeldy   (Aberfeldy)
John Dewar and Sons Limited built this distillery near to the River Tay in 1897. It is licensed to John Dewar and Sons Limited, a D.C.L. subsidiary. The single malt whisky produced goes almost entirely to the blenders.

Blair Athol   (Pitlochry)
This distillery is unusual in that it is not sited in the village after which it was named but ten miles further south in Pitlochry. It was established in 1826 by a Mr. Conacher and was bought by the present owner Arthur Bell and Sons Limited in 1933. It is a small distillery tucked into a wooded hillside, in picturesque surroundings. The spring water from Ben Vrackie supplies all that is required for the distillery and the single malt whisky distilled which is bottled at 80 degrees proof is considered a good Highland malt. The distillery is sited in a tourist centre with many diverse attractions such as the Pitlochry Festival Theatre and a Salmon Ladder. The Pitlochry Pipe Band often entertains visitors to this

beautifully positioned distillery which is thoroughly geared to welcome visitors.

Deanston (near Doune)
Built on the site of an old cotton mill on the banks of the River Teith, the distillery is named after the village of Deanston, one mile to the west of Doune. Although it is near to the river, which is good for salmon, the water for the distillery comes from the Trossachs. It was acquired by Deanston Distilleries Limited, Glasgow, in 1969, a subsidiary of Invergordon Distillers Limited. The Highland malt whisky distilled is bottled at 70 degrees proof and marketed as *Deanston Mill*.

Edradour (Pitlochry)
This distillery was built in 1837 beside a burn with steep banks at the foot of the hill on land leased from the Duke of Atholl. It is the smallest distillery in Scotland, and the spirit-still holds under 500 gallons. It is now controlled by William Whiteley & Company, London, who are notable for their *House of Lords* and *King's Ransom* blends. The bulk of the Highland single malt whisky distilled is used for blending.

Glencadam (close to Brechin)
Glencadam Distillery was built in a deep sided Glen in 1825. It gets ample water supplies from the Moorfoot Loch. Now controlled by George Ballantine and Son Limited, a subsidiary of Hiram Walker and Sons (Scotland) Limited, the entire whisky production is used for blending.

Glenturret (2 miles north-west of Crieff)
Situated on the banks of the Turret water which rises on Ben Chonzie (3,048 ft.) and joins the River Earn, this distillery is supposed to date back to the illicit distilling days in the late 18th century. The Highland single malt whisky distilled is unusual and only easily obtainable from the Glenturret Distillery Limited, Crieff.

Hillside (Montrose)
Founded in the 19th century, this distillery was acquired by William Sanderson in the 1890's. One of the only two distilleries in Montrose sometimes called the 'Venice of the North', it has no difficulties in obtaining water since the town

supply is good enough to be used. Licensed to William Sanderson & Sons, Limited, South Queensferry, West Lothian, blenders of *Vat 69*, it is a D.C.L. subsidiary. The entire output is used for blending.

Lochside

See entry under Lochside on page 50, Chapter 6.

North Port   (Brechin)

This second distillery in Brechin, was founded by the Guthrie Brothers in 1820. Water is piped from the Grampian Mountains and peat is obtained from the same source. It is now licensed to J. & G. Stewart of Leith, a subsidiary of the D.C.L. The whisky produced is used entirely for blending.

Tullibardine   (close to Gleneagles)

Originally a brewery which was reputedly amongst the oldest in Scotland, it was converted into a distillery in 1949. It gets its water supplies from the Danny Burn. The distillery was acquired by Invergordon Distillers Limited in 1971 and the whisky distilled is a fine Highland single malt bottled at 5 and 10 years and 70 degrees proof.

APPENDIX
AND
LIST OF ILLUSTRATIONS

Appendix

Notable Distillers, Blenders and Blends

Aberlour-Glenlivet Distillery Company, Aberlour, Grampian Region
   Distillery: Aberlour-Glenlivet
Ardbeg Distillery Company, Islay
   Distillery: Ardbeg (Islay)
Barton Distilling (Scotland), Alexandria, Strathclyde Region
   Distilleries: Littlemill; Loch Lomond   Blend: *House of Stewart*
Arthur Bell & Sons, Perth
   Distilleries: Blair Atholl; Dufftown-Glenlivet; Inchgower; Pittyvaich-Glenlivet   Blends: *Bell's Extra Special; de luxe 12 year old*
Ben Nevis Distillery Company, Fort William
   Distillery: Ben Nevis
Distillers Company Limited, 12 Torphichen Street, Edinburgh
   Distilleries: Aberfeldy; Aultmore; Balmenach; Banff; Benrinnes; Benromach; Caledonian; Cambus; Cameronbridge; Caol Ila; Cardow; Carsebridge; Clynelish; Coleburn; Convalmore; Cragganmore; Craigellachie; Dailuaine; Dallas-Dhu; Dalwhinnie; Glen Albyn; Glendullan; Glen Elgin; Glenkinchie; Glenlochy; Glenlossie; Glen Mhor; Glentauchers; Glenury-Royal; Hillside; Imperial; Knochdhu; Lagavulin; Linkwood; Mannochmore; Millburn; Mortlach; North Port; Oban; Ord; Port Dundas; Port Ellen; Rosebank; Royal Brackla: Royal Lochnagar; Speyburn; St. Magdalene; Talisker; Teaninich   Blends: *Antiquary; Abbots Choice; Black & White; Dewars; Crawfords; Haig; Harvey's Gold Label; King George IV; Old Parr; Old Rarity; Usher's Green Stripe; Vat 69; Johnnie Walker; White Horse*
Eadie Cairns, 11, Bothwell Street, Glasgow, C. 2
   Distillery: Auchentoshan   Blends: *Cairns; B.C.*
Glendeveron Distillers Limited, Macduff, Grampian Region
   Distillery: Macduff
Glenturret Distillery Company, Crieff, Tayside Region
   Distillery: Glenturret

J. & G. Grant, Ballindalloch, Grampian Region
    Distillery: Glenfarclas-Glenlivet

William Grant & Sons, 206–8, West George Street, Glasgow, C2
    Distilleries: Balvenie; Girvan; Glenfiddich; Ladyburn
    Blends: *Standfast; Best Procurable*

Highland Distilleries Company, 107, West Nile Street, Glasgow, C.1
    Distilleries: Bunnahabhain; Glenglassaugh; Glengoyne; Glenrothes-Glenlivet; Highland Park; Tamdhu-Glenlivet Blends: *Red Hackle; Lang's; Mak Readie; Scottish Cream*

International Distillers & Vintners, 1, York Gate, London NW1 4PU
    Distilleries: Auchroisk; Glen Spey; Knockando; Strathmill Blends: *J. & B. Rare; Spey Royal*

Invergordon Distillers: Invergordon, Highland Region
    Distilleries; Bruichladdich; Deanston; Invergordon; Tamnavulin; Tullibarine Blend: *Findlater's Finest*

Inverhouse Distillers; Moffat Distilleries, Airdrie
    Distilleries: Bladnoch; Moffat Blends: *Macarthurs; Inverhouse*

Ledaig Distillery Company, Tobermory, Isle of Mull, Strathclyde Region
    Distillery: Ledaig (Tobermory)

Long John International, 20, Queen Anne's Gate, London SW1H 9AA (Seager Evans is a subsidiary)
    Distilleries: Kinclaith: Glenugie; Laphroaig; Tormore; Strathclyde Blends: *Long John; Long John 12 year old; Islay Mist*

Macallan-Glenlivet Limited, Craigellachie, Grampian Region
    Distillery: Macallan-Glenlivet

Macdonald & Muir: Queen's Dock, Leith, Edinburgh EH6 6NN
    Distilleries: Glenmorangie; Glen Moray-Glenlivet
    Blends: *Highland Queen; Highland Queen Grand 15*

MacNab: Lochside Distillery, Montrose
    Distillery: Lochside

J. A. Mitchell: Campbeltown
    Distillery: Springbank

Stanley P. Morrison & Co. 13, Royal Crescent, Glasgow, C3
    Distilleries: Bowmore; Glengarioch

North British Distillery Company, Wheatfield Road, Edinburgh EH11 2PX
    Distillery: North British
North of Scotland Distilling Company, Cambus, Central Region
    Distillery: Strathmore
Seagram Distillers Limited, 111–113 Renfrew Road, Paisley PA3 4DY
    Distilleries: Glen Keith-Glenlivet; Strath Isla-Glenlivet; Braes of Glenlivet Blends: *Chivas Regal; Royal Salute; Royal Strathythan; 100 Pipers; Four Crown*
Scottish & Newcastle Breweries, 11 Holyrood Road, Edinburgh EH8 8AY
    Distilleries: Isle of Jura; Glenallachie Blends: *Mackinlays; MacPherson's Cluny*
William Teacher & Sons, 14 St. Enoch Square, Glasgow G1 4BZ
    Distilleries: Ardmore; Glendronach Blend: *Highland Cream*
The Glenlivet Distillers Limited, 45 Frederick Street, Edinburgh EH2 1YG
(Hill Thomson, 45 Frederick Street, Edinburgh are a subsidiary)
    Distilleries: Benriach-Glenlivet; Caperdonich; Glen Grant-Glenlivet; Longmorn-Glenlivet; The Glenlivet Blends: *Queen Anne; Something Special; St. Leger*
Tomatin Distillers Company, Limited, 34 Dover Street, London W1X 4HX
    Distillery: Tomatin Blend: *Big T*
Hiram Walker & Sons (Scotland) Limited, 3 High Street, Dumbarton G82 1ND
    Distilleries: Balblair; Dumbarton; Glenburgie; Glencraig; Inverleven; Lomond; Miltonduff; Mosstowie; Pulteney; Scapa Blends: *Ballantine's; Ambassador; Old Smuggler*
William Whiteley & Company, Atlas House, 57a Catherine Place, London SW1E 6HA
    Distillery: Edradour Blends: *House of Lords; Kings Ransom*
Whyte & Mackay, 50 Wellington Street, Glasgow G2 6EE
    Distillery: Dalmore Blends: *Whyte & Mackay's Special; Supreme; 21 years old*

List of Illustrations